Saturday's Boys

The Football Experience

Saturday's Boys

The Football Experience

EDITED BY
HARRY LANSDOWN AND ALEX SPILLIUS

Willow Books
Harper Collins

Willow Books
William Collins Sons & Co Ltd
London · Glasgow · Sydney · Auckland · Toronto · Johannesburg

First published in 1990
© Harry Lansdown and Alex Spillius 1990

A CIP CATALOGUE RECORD FOR THIS BOOK IS AVAILABLE FROM THE BRITISH LIBRARY

ISBN 0 00 218384 6

Designed by Judith Gordon
Typeset by Ace Filmsetting Ltd, Frome
Printed and bound in Great Britain by
William Collins Sons & Co Ltd, Glasgow

To our Dads
for taking us in the first place

CONTENTS

Acknowledgements

The editors would like to thank the following for their time, kindness, assistance and advice:

Helen Armitage

Peter Ball

Kate Barker

Barry Brennan

Nicky Brodie

Charles Burgess

Colin Cameron

Michael Clive

Richard Cohen

Bernard Davy

Jim Ferguson

Kim Fletcher

Alex Gardiner

Juliet Gardiner

Willis Hall

Tom Horan

Richard Jobson

Chris Jones

Richard Lansdown

John Moynihan

Paul Newman

Rowena O'Connell

Jack Rollin

Phil Shaw

Carrie Smilg

Elizabeth Spillius

Jim Spillius

Sara Spillius

Rogan Taylor

Gillian Tindall

Introduction

After an hour or so's conversation at the Greyhound Pub, Hendon, *Saturday's Boys* was born. Strangely, we had both had the same idea at the same time, though on reflection perhaps the coincidence was not that surprising. As then trainee reporters on the *Hendon & Finchley Times*, we had become friends because there was no one else who would tolerate our incessant connoisseurs' football chat. During arguments on such weighty matters as Pat Nevin's tastes in music and Coventry City's history of away strips (one of them *was* brown), some things were agreed on: football deserved a richer literature, with more alternatives to the tradition of impersonal and blandly written histories and biographies.

It struck us that amid the game's problems, which sicken people and turn them away, it has become easy to forget why anyone ever went to football matches in the first place. There are troubles, and there have been crises, but the sport is still the national game, permeating society to a greater extent than any others.

We asked a variety of people, most of whom do not make a living out of the game, to write about what football means to them. Professional expertise was not a qualification, enthusiasm for football and honest writing were.

Freddie Ayer was the first to agree to contribute and his eagerness guaranteed the project stayed alive early on. Sadly, the great philosopher and Spurs supporter died soon afterwards. He would have loved grappling with the question – why football?, and recalling the glories of Tottenham teams. It turned out, however, that there was no shortage of volunteers to put their names to the book even before a publisher had been found. People said yes. Why? Because they wanted the rare opportunity to expand on their favourite sport for several thousand words. A chance to say, this is what football feels like.

The writers share a lifetime attachment to football; the sort of attachment that makes Saturday a different day of the week – the day when the buzz created by going to a match paradoxically makes everything else seem irrelevant yet more valuable. Or if circumstances prevent actually going, followers find themselves itching to be by a radio or television at 4.45 p.m. to see how their team have got on. This attachment tends to stay, in one guise or another, for life.

It's an attachment that is in most cases made young and among boys, so apologies to Kate Hoey, our only female writer, for our title *Saturday's Boys*. One in twenty is probably the ratio of women to men at most matches – if only more women went it would help make the grounds better places.

The answer to why this obsession takes such a grip is elusive, but our writers grapple boldly with it. All supporters have a golden period, or player, and some of the chapters are devoted to this, while others describe the author's playing history, whether as a hopeful schoolboy trialist, or Sunday parks player fascinated by his own ineptitude. Others talk of how football entwined with their personal and family lives, while a couple join in the ancient (and fully justified) supporter's right to moan about the way their beloved club is run. There is a variety of experience with a common denominator: taking pleasure in having football own a part of one's life.

Football post-Hillsborough will never be the same and the tragedy should not be forgotten. But that horrific day uncovered a dignity among supporters few outside the game can have realized existed. The sport cannot be written off or legislated into a punier existence. You cannot say the game is in decline to an Aston Villa or Oldham fan, or to the supporters of Colne Dynamo who have seen their team rise from one non-league division to another year upon year; or to someone who has just scored the winning goal in the 76th minute of a crucial Sunday league match for nobody in particular. Playing, supporting and dreaming, and dreaming, supporting and playing: participation is the British football experience.

There is scarcely a mention of hooliganism in the chapters that follow. No one has written about it, though all have witnessed it at some point. Fighting is not really part of most people's Saturdays. It is an ugly, small-minded aside, indulged in by a minority, that is hyped up out of all proportion by people, many of whom do not go to football except in search of it.

The trouble with football fans is not that they are all hooligans. Their problem is they love the game too much, and in the past haven't been critical enough of the way they are treated. But times are changing. Rogan Taylor and friends have launched the Football Supporters'

Association, a radical idea breaking down the partisanship of fans to get them some say in the running of the game.

Fanzines are another forward step. Clubs don't like them because they dare to criticize, but the patronizing, boring Pravda-type programme, where the manager's notes tell you to cheer on the lads and nothing else, now has a rival publication. There are three fanzine writers in this collection because fanzines are now part of football.

Problems exist in the game and need to be dealt with, but it is still the players and the matches that followers talk about to each other most. Soon the agents or the possibility of a superleague seems irrelevant compared to the nitty gritty of 'are we going to win?' and 'why is so-and-so playing *again?*'. The outstanding teams and players are never forgotten. English football is clearly suffering from having been banned from European club competition, and we seem more isolated than ever with our over-emphasis on speed and endurance. But still, in today's First Division there is a band of individualists, led by John Barnes, who stand out amidst the mediocrity. Players like Matthew Le Tissier, Paul Parker, Des Walker, Nigel Clough, David Rocastle, Paul Gascoigne and Tony Daley have yet to prove themselves fully; but on their good days they remain in the supporters' thoughts long after the rest of the match has become a blur.

The secretary of the PFA, Gordon Taylor, absorbed in trying to solve football's problems, once said: 'Sometimes I wonder how the game survives.' We hope *Saturday's Boys* has provided some of the answers.

Harry Lansdown
Alex Spillius

Simon Inglis

Simon has risen to prominence through his quirky, detailed research into football stadia, and is now a cult figure among supporters – celebrated for his knowledge, his enthusiasm, and the fervent delivery of his opinions. In 1988, between writing The Football Grounds of Great Britain *and* The Football Grounds of Europe, *Simon was chosen as the Football League's official centenary historian, an eccentric but honourable role for someone who previously taught modern history in London.*

Remember the Sabbath Day to Keep It Holy

SIMON INGLIS

Yippee ya yayhhh,
Yippee ya yohhhh,
Holte Enders in the skyeee . . .

I thought that I'd grow out of it. That with the retreat of my teenage acne and the retirement of Brian Little I'd not care quite so much.

I imagined that, in time, all the misgivings I'd secretly nurtured on the terraces would eventually form themselves into a rational argument in favour of total abstention. Maturity, wisdom, responsibility even, would find me walking slowly away from Villa Park one autumn evening, the towers of Aston Hall a shadowy silhouette in the twilight. Roy Orbison would be singing his mournful lament, 'It's Over', as I passed the Holte pub for the last time, draped my claret and blue scarf over a railing, then paused for one last look at the floodlights before walking off into the sunset beyond Spaghetti Junction. A Brummie urchin would try to press on me a *Sports Argus*, hot off the press. 'But Simey,' he would cry out nasally, as I denied him, 'Worrabout the Midland Combination results? Worrabout the hours you've spent scanning the Southern League lineups to see what former Villa players have fallen on hard times? Worrabout . . .'

But I'd moved on. Sorry boys, you're on your own now. I'm busy. I'm going to university. I'm going to live in Israel and make the desert bloom. I'm going to play drums for the Rolling Stones and take drugs on the Marrakesh Express. The Holte End is no place for a budding Jewish Socialist intellectual with shoulderlength hair and flapping flares fit to floor a passing mastiff.

The misgivings were many, but what they essentially boiled down to was the question, 'What's a boy like you doing in a place like this?' Having fun? Letting off steam? Yeh yeh, we know all about that. But while all around me there were youths in steel-capped boots making monkey noises every time Laurie Cunningham or Cyrille Regis got the ball, it was easy to feel alienated. Perhaps I should get out quick before the mob turned on me – the one with the Villa scarf hiding his yellow star.

At Leeds I saw the veins stand out on a hundred pale white necks as a group of the home fans contorted their bodies forward to spit curses and hate towards Villa's black winger, Mark Walters. I thought their blood vessels would burst with the effort. In fact I was only attacked once, in Birmingham City Centre, and it was only my scarf they wanted. 'Take it,' I whimpered. Other times I just ran.

I was also threatened with eviction from the Baseball Ground for saying 'Shit' when Derby scored. My refined middle-class accent ensured my freedom. On the way home some Villa fans became bored and decided to dismantle the train. The police passed through each carriage, grabbing young male passengers arbitrarily, then lined up their suspects on the station platform. I was among them.

'Who knows anything about the damage?' a senior bobby demanded. I knew nothing – honest – but blushed with guilt anyway, so I spent the rest of the journey locked in a cage in the guard's van, pressed up against a hundred or so burly, beery hardnuts with enough tattoos between them to decorate a Zeppelin. How they laughed and crowed in front of the yapping police Alsatians, while I, a mere thirteen-year-old, wiped my hot stinging eyes, imagined myself on a cattle truck to Auschwitz and foresaw a brilliant future shattered by a spell in borstal and parental rejection.

The police told us we'd all have our names taken and our fathers summoned to New Street Station to collect us from custody. Turning on the middle-class voice again I pleaded through the cage bars. 'Look officer, I appreciate your dilemma, but you've made a terrible mistake.' God must have heard my cry of pain, because at New Street, miraculously, we were all released unconditionally. Shaking with relief and indignation I sped home to tell my parents the whole tale. Worldly wise as ever, their reaction was calm. Life's rich tapestry and all that.

I don't think I've ever possessed what may be termed 'a footballing brain'. Although I played avidly and understood all the rules, I was always disturbed by its apparent cruelty and fickle nature. For example, how could Tommy Docherty have changed Villa's strip in the face of eighty or more years of tradition? How could Bruce Rioch and John Gidman have left Villa for another club? Did we not love them enough? And why does Vic Crowe not still work for Villa? He seemed such a nice man. Most incomprehensible of all, how on earth was it possible that Lionel Martin – nine goals in forty-four appearances, the sweetest little ball player since George Best – never quite established himself in the first team and was eventually consigned to non-league football? Don't talk to me about work rate or behind-the-scenes disagreements. Lionel looked good in a Villa shirt (the traditional one that is). He once scored a header against Spurs, outjumping Mike England, even though he was a foot or so smaller.

I must therefore assume that he didn't attain stardom because of his name. Maybe if he'd been a Bobby, or a Steve or a Mike it would have been easier. But a Lionel, or a Simon for that matter, stood no chance. I certainly was never destined to make my mark in the football world. I didn't like heading the ball, for a start. It always seemed to hurt.

Not for me a few pints before the game or a boozy train journey to away games. For me, going to a match has always been more of a spiritual release – a time for reflection, a time for solitary concentration with just the occasional 'Hallelujah' and 'Hosannah in the Top Corner of the Net'. Even on that May afternoon in 1981 when Villa won the League Championship, when I stood at the Clock End at Arsenal, hardly comprehending the enormity of what had occurred, I just could not bring myself to join in with the reverent chants of, 'Saunders, Saunders, Saunders, Saunders . . .'. Not because I disliked either the tune ('Amazing Grace') or the manager in question, but because the slavish acclaim of one individual raised alarm bells in my brain. This, I imagined, was the road to Nuremberg. To submerge my persona in the tide of adulation was to conform with Hannah Arendt's 'notion of superfluousness', in which individuals abdicate their sense of self when called to rally for the cause. It would have been no different had it been the Queen, Ken Livingstone, or even Pelé. I would not die for my country, right or wrong. I would not worship the Claret and Blue shirt, no matter who wore it (not even Lionel Martin). If indeed I was one of Montesquieu's 'flexible beings', one who is equally capable of both knowing his own mind and being robbed of it, I would be on my guard. *On* the Holte End, but not *of* it.

7

And if I wasn't transported back to Nuremberg then often I wasn't transported at all. There have been times when I have stood, or more recently sat down, and thought to myself, 'Life is too short. Ninety minutes is too long.' After all, between Brian Little and David Platt there was a long gap.

For a while I even put about the theory that the reason most people go to football matches is that they have precious little else to do on a Saturday afternoon. Naturally this pithy little observation – delivered so eruditely to my clever friends (how they laughed!) – did not apply to me. Oh no, there were a thousand and one things to do on a Saturday afternoon – writing, shopping, DIY, exhibitions and . . . er, well, plenty of things. Believe me, I've tried them all.

> *When I was young my father said,*
> *Son I have something to say.*
> *Happy to be a Villa fan,*
> *Until your dying day.*

My father's message was somewhat different from the Holte End's, which is why I spent almost every Saturday morning in synagogue, biting my nails and fretting over the events of the ensuing afternoon. Once, on *Yom Kippur*, the most solemn day of the Jewish calendar, the Day of Atonement no less, I slipped a few football programmes inside my prayer book to stave off the boredom. For some reason they were Coventry City programmes; Bill Glazier, Mick Coop, Dietmar Bruck, Ernie . . . I got caught. I bit my nails. Remember the Second Commandment, 'Thou shalt have no other gods before me'. I once persuaded myself, during another ponderous sermon by the rabbi with wet lips, that I held Tommy Docherty in higher esteem than the Almighty. The proof of Tommy's existence, I reasoned, was at least self-evident. Besides which, why couldn't a fourteen-year-old formulate beliefs of his own. To me, adults seemed to be racked by doubts about God and their faith. I had no such qualms – at least, not until Docherty changed Villa strip and we were, *ipso facto*, relegated to the Third Division.

Saturday lunchtime. After synagogue, sweet *Kiddush* wine and having my nose tugged playfully by old ladies in fox-furs – '*Good Shabbos, Good Shabbos*', but please, Oh God no, no kisses! – Sabbath meals at home with the family were sacrosanct.

They were torture. Not because of my family or the food. I loved them both and still do. But would I get away in time? If visitors were invited, would the Sabbath meal be dragged out? If, God forbid, the rabbi came to lunch, would the prayers take longer? There were voices in my head, the voices of the Holte End, calling out, 'Come on Simon – clap clap – Come on Simon . . .'

And then there were the taunts from around the table.

'Don't get there too early, Simon. They might ask you to play.'

By 1.15 p.m. I'd be anxious. If it stretched to 1.30 p.m. I was frantic; snatching away dishes from my brother and sister as soon as they'd finished, clearing the table so rapidly that if anyone asked for seconds I'd have to go back into the kitchen and retrieve their plates. When the final blessed 'Amen' was sung at the climax of Grace After Meals (always pronounced in best Anglo-Hebrew as 'O Main') I had to sit for just long enough not to offend anyone – perhaps folding my napkin with a sigh and an 'ah well' – before leaping up like Billy Whizz, kissing the by-now bemused parents (who never ever stopped me), grabbing the woolly scarf and, despite the *gefilte* fish and *lockshen* pudding floating warmly around inside me on a lake of chicken soup, sprinting like a demon to the number 50 bus stop on Moseley Road.

'Now look over there, young Ben. Watch that kid go!'

'Wowee! if I could run like that I'd win a Gold at the Olympics, for sure.'

'Forget it Ben. You gotta be real desperate to move that fast.'

Fighting the stitch and the clock I'd run, along Forest Road, crossing into Woodbridge Road, stopping only at Hinton's for the afternoon's confectionery. Please God, don't let there be an old lady in front of me at the counter. Please God, Mr Hinton hasn't run out of Benson's blackcurrant and liquorice. For what I am about to receive, may the Lord make me truly spotty.

The number 50 bus took the back way into town, which meant skirting the edges of Birmingham City territory: mean streets, ugly warehouses, slums, railway arches. From the top deck I looked out with the contempt of a Bourbon prince passing through the Faubourg St Antoine. No way did I covet my neighbour's house – St Andrew's, City's proletarian bunker of a ground. Nor his ox, nor his ass, nor his Johnny Vincent nor his Fred Pickering. In fact, who were these awful, common people in their all-blue 'modern' kit who kept doing better than Villa and concocting pathetic mascots like Beau Brummie and, and signing heart-throb players like Trevor Hockey and, and singing 'Keep right on to the end of the road' with such gusto and, and who bloody signed John Sleewenhoek, OUR centre half, when he was at his peak, and, and, and, and . . .

> *F--- off West Brom and Birmingham,*
> *F--- off West Brom and Birmingham,*
> *And Birmingham,*
> *And Birmingham,*
> *And Birmingham,*
> *And Birmingham.*

The Holte End was right.

Once in town the bus would pull up in Carrs Lane outside M & S. Then came another sprint, this time a dodging, weaving effort, mostly uphill and through streets and arcades crowded with shoppers – and who did they think they were, on a Saturday afternoon? – until reaching the lines of blue and cream Villa Park special buses at the top of Corporation Street. The moment I slumped, heavy breathing but exultant, onto the itchy moquette bench seats of those softly rolling old Guy Arab double-deckers, I felt the embrace of a familiar belonging. The haze of tobacco smoke (to which in time I would contribute from my illicit pack of ten Number Six), the expectant chatter, the Brummie accents, the parade of weathered faces and rough hands – this was my *liaison dangereuse*. I was out of school, out of uniform, out among Villa boys, out – gulp – among the working classes.

I was alone, excluded from their banter by my vowels and isolated from their meaning by my education. I could look, but I could not touch my fellow travellers. Nor could I share their easy frivolity. I was an Essene in the midst of Sadducees.

For no one on these grinding, heavy buses, no one, loved Aston Villa as much as I, nor suffered for them as greatly. No one else, surely, sensed the confluence of time – one Saturday afternoon, and yet a hundred years of this great city: the Victorian Gothic pomp of municipal Birmingham as we rolled and swayed downhill past the law courts on Corporation Street; the Hockley sweat-shops; Summer Lane, where in the 1880s draper William McGregor had toyed with the idea of a Football League; the ATV Studios where Janice Nicholls 'Gave it

Foive'; then Ansell's brewery at Aston Cross, and the HP Sauce factory with its sickly fumes. This was another Birmingham, a Birmingham which has since been destroyed and a Birmingham which I sometimes ache for when I return, even though it was almost gone by the time I was born into it.

I wanted it to be foggy. I wanted to be on a trolley bus, or even better, a tram. I wanted to be en route to see Pongo Waring hit a brace against Herbert Chapman's Arsenal. I wanted England to be my England, the England of Ealing Studios, and for Birmingham to be Joseph Chamberlain's; iron railings and municipal parks, black Morris Minors and steamy tea-rooms at Snow Hill Station. Son Neville would have stopped Hitler in his tracks, the new look tacky Bull Ring would have stayed on the drawing board, along with the box-like, one-man operated, Atlantean and Fleetline buses. I would have married Shula Archer, Lionel Martin would have played for England. My school wouldn't have played bloody rugby, Rachel Cohen would have let me undo her bra and . . . here we were, at the bus terminus by the edge of Aston Park, leaping down the stairs off the open platform of the Guy Arab.

By now I would be as crazed with anticipation as was humanly possible without actually wetting myself. Villa Park was in sight, and yet I could only reach it as quickly as my legs would carry me.

An hour before kick off.

Don't start without me!

I don't think anyone associated with Villa in the late 1960s and early 1970s has ever fully appreciated the crucial effect my own experiences had upon the team's performances.

If, for example, I arrived at Villa Park any time after 2 p.m. some malicious interloper was bound to have usurped my spot on the terraces (Holte End, front of the middle tier, slightly to the left of the goal). In that unthinkable event, it followed that the game's co-ordinates in the space-time continuum would almost certainly be sent spiralling into the void, probably to re-emerge in the twenty-first century as a Birmingham City v Walsall reserve match (Gobi Desert, kick-off Thursday at 9.15 a.m.). Ley-lines would curl up in horror, Venus would collide with Mars and you could bet Keith Bradley would give away a penalty in the first 10 minutes. And unknown to anyone, it would all be my family's fault for being such slow eaters on the Sabbath.

Or if I didn't have time to read the *Villa News and Record* (plus, for a while, the inserted *Football League Review* – would Villa's goalkeeper Colin Withers ever oust George Best from the Top Ten poll of best-looking players?), then there was always the risk that my discomfort would somehow be transmitted to the Villa team, and, like tennis players facing a serve only to be distracted by a fly, they would want to cry out, 'Hold it ref, Simon's not ready!' But the referee would never listen and then Villa would lose and again it would be all my family's fault for eating so slowly.

And if you don't bloody well believe me, just look at the results from that period. We lost all the bloody time. And when I got home my family would be cowering in the living room in front of Dr Who, gauging how badly Villa had performed by the ferocity with which the front door was slammed and whether I went in to say hello or just stormed up to my bedroom, hands stained in ink from the *Argus*, clothes stinking of salt and vinegar. And I wasn't bloody crying. I wasn't. I just had something in my eye.

Not even my elder brother was an ally. He'd been with me at my first ever match, on 21 April 1962. One of Dad's patients had some spare season tickets in the Trinity Road Stand and, at the age of seven, I was driven away from suburban Moseley to the solemn grandeur of Aston, with its park, its church and graveyard, its narrow streets with terraced houses and the red bricks of Villa Park itself.

That afternoon I learned my first swear word and saw Villa beat Leicester 8–3. Derek Dougan for Villa sported a sort of pre-Tony Daley Mohican haircut, and I think Charlie Aitken did a rugby tackle on a Leicester player. I don't recall much else except an inkling that Gordon Banks might have been in goal for Leicester. Certainly the high score didn't seem at all exceptional. Weren't Villa always meant to thrash the opposition?

But even if Villa had lost that afternoon it would have made no difference. Villa Park had class. It had history. It had eccentric buildings in odd places. It had iron railings and a bowling green. Villa Park was a symbol of the old Birmingham of my sepia-tinted imagination.

*

I have been visiting football grounds ever since, and for a while now I have been writing about them. 'The best job in the world,' some fans say to me. For five years I also wrote about what happened inside them, for *The Guardian* newspaper.

It was almost the perfect antidote.

On the terraces I could be alone – just me and the Villa, in holy communion. In the press box it was different. I was a neutral, a profes-sional neutral. No cheering, no hysterics. Stay seated when glorious goals are scored and just mutter appreciatively. Just who passed to whom, when, how, and with what result. Some of my fellow scribes treated me benignly, and I made a few friends. But the majority ignored me and I ignored them.

'Chap with the big nose and glasses? *Guardian* by the looks of it.'

One or two, judging by the tenor of their press box comments on black players, might even have alluded to my racial origins.

I soon gave up asking the managers any questions. Of one I inno-cently enquired whether a switch of wingers at half-time had been a tactical ploy. I was told, in return, 'My lads gave 110 per cent and I couldn't ask any more than that.' In the crowded corridor at Anfield which quaintly doubles as an interview room I asked Bob Paisley if he was worried about a particularly uncharacteristic lapse in defence which had cost Liverpool a goal.

'Goal? What goal?' he spat back at me, and then, playing to the gallery, he appealed to the other dozen or so reporters, 'Did any of you lot see a goal?'

Of course they had. It was a matter of record. Yet they all shook their heads in denial. Then turning back to me, his power affirmed by the cowed assemblage, Paisley sneered, 'You'll never make a bloody football reporter asking questions like that, my lad.'

As I recoiled into the background, blushing deeper than even Paisley's ruddy complexion, I realized at once that he was right. I couldn't adapt to the circuit, and in 1986 I went back to the terraces, grateful for the anonymity it provided and happy not to have to record who passed to whom, when, how and with what result. Having heard what the players and managers had to say for themselves I decided I no longer wanted to know. Unlike the child bedazzled by a magician's sleight of hand, I had lost my desire to learn how the trick was per-formed. Seeing was believing, was enough.

Maturity, wisdom, responsibility even – I have dallied with all three. And now, halfway through my allotted three-score and ten I have come to the quite sober conclusion that there is nothing else I would rather do on a Saturday afternoon. A weekend without the Villa is like a bag of chips without salt and vinegar: worth savouring but ultimately bland and anti-climactic.

Times change. I live in London and I don't hate the Blues any more. There are no more football specials from Corporation Street, no more Guy Arabs, the Ansell's brewery has gone, Aston Cross has become a no-man's land, and whole swathes of Birmingham have been lost to fast roads, grass verges and quick-build industrial units.

I miss a lot of games too. Really miss them.

I miss the two Bardolph-like brothers on the Holte End with their shiny noses and hip flasks. I miss the man who used to light up fat cigars at the beginning of each half. If you asked him how long there was to go he'd look at his glowing stub and say, 'Bout 8 minutes.'

But there are other joys. Football fans are a reassuringly ordinary bunch really. I feel quite at home with them now, especially the Villa crowd with their dry wit and well-honed irony. 'Always look on the bright side of life, doo-doo, doo-doo, doo-doo . . .' they sing. At one particularly dire match recently I heard someone call out in the eerie silence, 'Paracetamol! Get your Paracetamol!'

I still bite my nails and I still hate it when Villa lose the toss and kick towards the Holte End in the first half. Sometimes I wonder about death and hope it will not come before a big game. To die and not know the outcome . . . I sometimes find myself on the terraces with my mind drifting far from the game, or skipping whole sections of the *Argus* I would have once devoured. I continue to have the nightmare in which I am running half naked towards Villa Park, well after three o'clock kick-off, only to find that the ground has become an indoor arena with no view of the pitch from what is left of the Holte End.

Sunday mornings haven't changed. Locked in the toilet I still peruse the Saturday results minutely: first Worcester City (where Lionel Martin ended up) and Chelmsford City (whose ground was the first I ever saw at the age of five). Then East Stirlingshire in the Scottish Second Division (because I've seen them twice and they're hopeless). Although I already know the details, my eyes always end up lingering upon the Villa result, as if it had no bearing until committed to print.

14

Attendance, current league placing, scorers and times. Own goals and penalties are an eyesore, and I prefer the forwards to score rather than the defenders. So much tidier.

Sometimes I find myself in the North Stand at Villa Park, standing up to cheer another David Platt or Tony Daley special, before turning to the man celebrating next to me. 'What a goal!' I shout above the din, and he beams back.

I always hoped Dad would come along one day and see what all the fuss was about. And I suppose he always knew that I'd never quite grow out of it.

Yippee ya yayhhh, Yippee ya yohhh . . .

Adrian Henri

If Adrian was a footballer he would be a manager's dream: the utility player. An accomplished painter, singer, songwriter and playwright, Adrian could be termed the Stevie Nicol of the arts world. But he is best known for his poetry and leading the poetry-rock group 'Liverpool Scene' from 1967 to 1970. His recent publications of poems include The Phantom Lollipop Lady *(1986)*, Wish You Were Here *(1990) and* Box *(1990)*.

The Glory that was Rome

ADRIAN HENRI

Tell me Ma, me Ma
I don't want no tea no tea
We're going to Italy
Tell me Ma, me Ma

The Kop, Anfield, 1977

The streets of Liverpool echoed with it, the streets of Rome were echoing with it. A fine evening in May 1977, Liverpool were going to beat Borussia Mönchengladbach at the Stadio Olimpico; we all knew that and a sizeable proportion of the population of the city had travelled here to see it happen; by car, by train, by bus and by plane. Almost impossible to imagine in these sad post-Heysel days, the sheer heady excitement of hearing yet another bit of the Kop choir as you walked past the Vittorio Emmanuele monument, the fun, the adrenalin, the humour: 'I'll meet you in the Vatican.' 'Where, the bar or the lounge?' Thousands of Scousers, 'Scallies' and businessmen, matrons from Southport and teenage girls from the Dingle. And not a single arrest. Riot police on every corner, an armoured car at the airport. Rome watched, bemused, amused and slightly uncomprehending. Two months earlier, Liverpool had been taken over by St Etienne supporters in much the same way: green and white scarves, clothes, banners everywhere, including, incredibly, lots of green Beatle wigs, which they thought a great joke. They were all over the place – I saw two of them giving wine to a street sweeper. The game that night was heart stopping, the most exciting I've ever been to. 'You'll Never Walk Alone' almost drowned out by 'Allez Les Verts' to the tune of 'Ave Maria'. The French champions led 1–0 from the first leg, and the away goals rule meant that until we finally made it 3–1 near the end the result was in the balance. In fact, I don't think either lot of supporters wanted to win then. It should have been Rocheteau and co. in Rome with us. In pubs and clubs all over town afterwards scarves, drinks and

17

addresses were swapped. I've never seen such real affection between fans, even Liverpool and Everton.

When we took our seats in the Olympic Stadium that May evening I noticed a lot of green and white scarves in the next block. Going over to investigate, I discovered there was a huge contingent of St Etienne fans: 'You beat us; so we've come to support you,' they explained. For some reason, the Kop had chosen Joey Jones as a sort of bogeyman (and this in a team that boasted Tommy Smith), and produced a wonderful series of banners that year. The first one read: JOEY EATS FROG'S LEGS. The next, for FC Zurich: JOEY MAKES THE SWISS ROLL. Now, unveiled across a whole block of seats, a huge red on white banner read: JOEY ATE THE FROG'S LEGS, MADE THE SWISS ROLL, NOW HE'S MUNCHING GLADBACHS.

They're a curious breed, Liverpool fans. For a start, they don't conform to the Thatcher/Moynihan stereotype. I wasn't by any means the only one exploring the art galleries and ancient monuments those two days. After a UEFA Cup game in Bruges, a red-scarved compatriot told me where to get the best lobsters in Ostend (he was right, too). Although I wasn't the only Liverpudlian in the art gallery there, either, I probably was the only one to make a pilgrimage to James Ensor's grave at St Marie-des-Mers. Nor am I alone in going to Anfield (or Goodison) in the afternoon and the Philarmonic Hall the same night.

I went to Rome the easy way – flight, ticket, two days hotel inclusive, along with lots of prosperous-looking (probably Conservative voting) businessmen and women taking the opportunity for a bit of tourism, good food and wine, as well as the game itself. It was, in fact, four such friends of mine (including an off-duty policeman) who were attacked after the next European Cup tie in Rome by knife-wielding Roman Ultras. An English disease? Try Ajax v Feyenoord.

I have happy memories of the Kop at their most inventive: singing 'Careless Hands' when Gary Sprake of Leeds United threw the ball into his own net; greeting Tommy Docherty, involved in a well publicized affair with a lady called Mary Brown, with a hilarious but unprintable version of 'Knees Up Mother Brown'. Like all Scousers, the Liverpool fan tends to have a cherished image of himself: rough diamond with a heart of gold, ready wit, outsinging the lot of 'em. Yet recently they've been regularly outsung by visiting supporters, and niggle at our players' mistakes (or supposed mistakes). They are, in fact, spoilt. We win everything, what's left to try for? The team do it, the fans somehow don't anymore. It's like occasionally offering Kit-E-Kat to a cat regularly fed on salmon and chicken.

But Rome '77 was undoubtedly our finest hour. A couple of weeks before the treble loomed: League Championship, FA Cup and European Cup. The last game of the season at Anfield, and a draw with West Ham United would win the league. The BBC had asked me to do a poem for television. Yes, I said, the usual fee plus two tickets, which were rarer than virgins at the Pierhead, where the Liver Birds are reputed to flap their wings whenever they spot one. So finally, I got to tread on the hallowed turf, overawed by the presence of the legendary Billy Liddell as well. I'd updated a poem called 'The Ballad of Chairman Shankly' for the occasion:

> The East is red, the West is red
> The North and South are too
> If you come from Leeds and Tottenham
> There's nothing you can do
> For the Blues are paper tigers
> And the southerners are worse . . .

It was a sort of blend of Kipling and one of those anthems in praise of Chairman Mao, using the names of all the players.

> And so the Great Leap forward starts
> The Heighway lies ahead
> With Keegan in the Hall of Fame
> And Toshack at the head
> The Smith a mighty man is he
> And Phil Neal rules the field
> And Callaghan is just the man
> Our team shall never yield.

But no tickets, so my girlfriend, Frances, and I hid inside the ground for a couple of hours, were lent a clipboard by the BBC team, and ended up sitting in the West Ham United dugout next to John Lyall, supposedly neutral, scarves hidden, and unable to shout.

The programme with my poem duly came out the day we lost the FA Cup to the loathed Manchester United. I was at Wembley. John and Guilda, landlord and landlady of our local pub, had hired a white Rolls-Royce for the occasion and we travelled with them, red scarves waving proudly in the wind from the windows. It didn't hurt any less at the time, but with hindsight there's some satisfaction in knowing that Manchester United have won hardly anything since. (There was a story going the rounds that when Nelson Mandela was released his first question was 'Have Manchester United won the League?') A year after the Cup Final, Wembley made amends when after a largely dull game we won the European Cup a second time by beating Bruges with a beautifully taken goal by Kenny Dalglish.

Now Frances and I were in Rome, walking round a corner towards the Colosseum. A cry went up from a corner café occupied by the Red Army. 'It's the poet!' I was plied with wine and perched on top of a table. 'Give us a poem.' So I did an impromptu reading right there:

> But Liverpool will ever rule
> 'Neath Paisley's mighty reign
> They grind their teeth in Germany
> In Italy and Spain.
>
> So fill the Cup and raise it up
> And drink three hearty cheers
> For the thoughts of Chairman Paisley
> Shall live a thousand years.

Uproar. Bemused waiters. It was better than the Library of Congress, better than the 1969 Isle of Wight festival.

We won, of course, 3–1. The amazing Simonsen for them, Terry McDermott, Tommy Smith and a Phil Neal penalty for us. McDermott's goal was immaculately taken, and by no means untypical of that gifted and often underrated player. A Tommy Smith goal was, it has to be said, a rather rarer event, but his stunning and unstoppable header took a lot of the fight out of the opposition. Kevin Keegan was everywhere, despite Berti Vogts following a bootlace length away. The joke going round the cafés the next morning was that, at the post-match party, every time Keegan got up to go to the bar, Vogts followed him.

As bar after bar closed, we ended up by a kiosk in a little square. A man came up. 'Great game'. 'Yeh great'. 'You're Adrian Henri.' Yes.

'Have a drink. You don't remember me, do you? I'm the flea man; I came to do your house last summer.' The cat had provoked the usual Liverpool 8 infestation that hot summer and here the Corpy flea man was, celebrating by a fountain in Rome.

The question often asked these days is how does the present Liverpool team compare with the great ones of the last twenty years? It's impossible to say; one has the impression that, if they could be tested against the rest of Europe, one might well feel this was the best ever; dominating the domestic game and winning the odd friendly isn't at all the same thing. I have the feeling that Liverpool today could go further than England in the World Cup.

Though Merseyside-born, I was brought up in North Wales, and spent my boyhood years watching Rhyl Athletic, with, I have to confess, a couple of visits to see Everton with a family friend from Liverpool. Later, as a student at Newcastle University, I watched the Magpies through the fabulous Cup-winning years of the early 1950s, with Wor Jackie, the Robledo brothers and co. Then, finally settling in Liverpool, I followed Liverpool in a desultory sort of way, my increasing involvement in performance meaning my weekends were often busy, and eventual full-time involvement in the music business meant that until after 1970 I simply wasn't free to go. The highlights of those early days were undoubtedly the games against Leeds. A friend of mine from Leeds said at the time that all those fixtures should have been played at Wembley.

What I find incredible, then as now, is the lack of appreciation of Liverpool and its players by southern-based writers and England team managers. When odd individuals are picked, they're often played out of position, or in unfamiliar roles. How often did the Thompson–Hughes central defensive partnership, the best I've ever seen, play for England? I don't think The Reds have ever been given credit for playing the nearest English equivalent to Dutch 'total football'; in that respect the present team *is* the best, with Rush and Grobbelaar virtually the only specialist players.

I suppose I idolize them all: Roger Hunt and Ian St John from the great Shankly teams. The elegance of Phil Thompson and the impetuosity of Emlyn Hughes. Kevin Keegan, the hardworking perfectionist; Dalglish giving the opposite impression to Keegan and relying on sheer natural ability, having those extra few seconds when everyone

21

else seemed to freeze-frame in the box. The single-minded Ian Rush, and now John Barnes, promptly christened 'tarmac' because he's the Black Heighway. And Steve Heighway himself. I suppose wingers are natural heroes. I was just too late for the Matthews–Finney era, but I used to watch Bobby Mitchell at Newcastle and I saw the incomparable George Best in his heyday.

But if I were to pick a favourite, it's the elegant, high-stepping Heighway. He was never really a favourite with the Anfield crowd, whom I think, considered him to be a bit work-and battle-shy, though I once watched him searching for the crown of a tooth in the mud after a game: he'd lost it scoring in a goalmouth scramble. Like Johnny Cash, Heighway was a great line-walker. He is a graduate of Warwick University, and was christened 'Big Bamber' by the rest of the two-graduate team to distinguish him from Brian Hall, a.k.a 'Little Bamber'. I often used to wonder if he'd ever seen me with 'Liverpool Scene', Warwick being one of our favourite venues. Eventually we met, improbably, judging a beauty contest: 'You don't know me, but I watch you every Saturday,' I remarked.

'And I watched *you* most Saturdays,' he replied.

Shortly before leaving Rome, we were sitting at a pavement café. A pretty young Italian woman with two children was standing at a bus stop nearby. A Liverpool supporter, obviously still celebrating, lurched over to her and started gesturing. Oh no, we thought, trouble. He went inside and returned a few minutes later with two enormous ice creams, which he handed solemnly to the children.

On the flight home, after the champagne had been emptied, we were about to come in to land at Speke Airport. A well-dressed, middle-aged man in front of us called the air hostess over:

'Hey, love, can you get the pilot to do a victory roll?'

Sebastian Faulks

Sebastian first showed his talents as a writer in May 1968, when as a fifteen-year-old he won three guineas for Football Monthly's *prize letter, on what football reveals about the British character. He has since turned his hand to lesser things, writing two highly acclaimed novels,* A Trick of the Light *(1984) and* The Girl at the Lion d'Or *(1989), as well as becoming deputy editor of* The Independent On Sunday. *A keen park footballer, his most memorable match is* The Independent's *4–0 Fleet Street league-winning triumph over* The Sun *in 1987.*

Upton and Other Parks

SEBASTIAN FAULKS

'Sorry, Strollers.'

Tim Jenkins, Guardian Strollers FC, goalkeeper. *Passim* 1980–8.

The team bus was winding through the plantations of Sri Lanka in 1981. We were on a cricket tour and one of the party was David Lacey, *The Guardian*'s football correspondent. Lacey is one of those people who lack the capacity to forget. His knowledge of films was more encyclopedic than that of either of the two professional film buffs on the trip, and when it came to football we used to cluster round him at the end of the coach to listen, like boys at a fruit machine.

'Okay, David,' I said. 'Name all eleven players in the West Ham team that won the FA Cup in 1964.'

'You'll have to give me a minute,' said Lacey, and closed his eyes in the tight concentration that preceded these spectacular feats. We watched the beautiful hills slide away beneath us and felt the coach swerve to avoid another bullock cart.

'Right,' said Lacey, and opened his eyes. 'Standen, Bovingdon, Birkett, Moore, Bond, Boyce, Peters, Brabrook, Byrne, Hurst, Sissons.'

Blimey. Even I sometimes had trouble remembering Bovingdon, and West Ham were my team. They had become so in that year, 1964, when I was eleven. Before that I had vaguely supported Spurs, because they were good, but not with the passion of ownership. So in the quarter-finals of the Cup I had decided that I was going to pick a team. West Ham seemed the right choice. No one else at school supported them; they were in the First Division, but near the bottom and thus in need of my support; and they were in the running for the Cup. I didn't know where West Ham was (Reading was our closest league team) and I had no idea that they had a reputation for classy, attacking football. I was lucky in my choice. One of my equally ignorant contemporaries picked Arsenal.

Three great years: the FA Cup in 1964; the Cup Winners' Cup in 1965; and in 1966 England won the World Cup, with, as everyone knows, Moore, Hurst and Peters. I felt I couldn't have picked a better team, even though we never did much in the league. When we played well, no one could touch us.

I didn't see West Ham in the flesh until 1967 when I went with a schoolfriend who was a Chelsea supporter. I stood next to a man with a cap who kept on shouting 'Come on, you Irons.' I didn't know what he was talking about, and it has always struck me as odd that an East End team should have a nickname which in cockney rhyming slang (iron hoof/poof) should lay them open to mockery, especially with such a shaky defence. There were plenty of exciting players on display that day. Hurst, Sissons and Peters for West Ham; Charlie Cooke, Tambling and Osgood for Chelsea. Yet it was to none of these that the eye was drawn, but to a defender: Bobby Moore. Much has been written about his style, but it was truly extraordinary. His anticipation was such that he seemed to be in a position to intercept a pass before the player on the other side had even decided to unload. He always gathered the ball moving forwards, so that at least three opposing players were wrong-footed and immediately had to go into reverse. Sometimes Moore would then step over the ball and turn the first challenger before releasing a 30-yard pass into the path of the winger; sometimes he would hit the ball flat and hard up to Ron Boyce ('Ticker' to the faithful) who would busy around the centre circle with it for a while before moving it on to Hurst or Peters.

Waves of applause rolled down towards Moore from the loving West Ham fans; every move he made was stamped with authority, every gesture made you certain he was the world's master of defence. Sometimes he could be almost too domineering; midfield players would lay the ball back to him when they might have taken it on. When he made the fatal mistake against Poland in the qualifying match for the 1974 World Cup, it was unbearable. The casual way he dragged the ball back inside to turn the tackler was a copy of the movement he had been successfully completing every Saturday for fifteen years. It was as if Denis Compton had been out at a crucial moment in a Test match to the sweep he had himself perfected. In my view that one error did nothing to tarnish Moore's career. On the contrary, by showing that he was human, like any other player, it made the riveting and masterful performances of his pomp seem all the more remarkable.

Even the Arsenal crowd was charmed. My first trip to Highbury came the following year. The ground made Upton Park look a bit down-market, to be honest. Arsenal had this greenhouse affair by the tunnel, the stadium was huge and, to a bright-eyed schoolboy, the red of their new shirts was dazzling. The Hammers looked all right, though. They played the better football, but their forwards kept getting chopped down by Simpson and Storey in the Arsenal defence. Even my Arsenal friend grimaced in embarrassment when Simpson was cautioned for another knee-high swing at West Ham's number 9.

This was a slow, gangling centre forward of about nineteen who had been brought in to replace Johnny Byrne. His name was Trevor Brooking and he had been in and out of the team for a couple of seasons. My reaction was 'Forget it'. Byrne was a real old centre forward with greased-back hair; he didn't play with a fag in the corner of his mouth, but it seemed implied. This youth Brooking was one-paced, kept falling over and didn't use his height in the air. 'Lovely build, that Brooking,' said the man next to me. 'That's about all,' I piped back bravely.

Time, Ron Greenwood and a hidden talent proved me wrong. Brooking became, with Keegan and Shilton, the light of his generation. Between the end of the Charlton era and the start of the Robson–Lineker age, these three were the only thing that made England worth watching. Yet Ron Greenwood's first move on being appointed England manager was to drop his old protégé. He brought in Ray Kennedy, a converted striker whose idea of creative midfield play was to gather the ball, then very slowly pass it to the opposition. Throughout his England career Brooking was accorded his place only grudgingly. If the manager could find a plodder – a Trevor Cherry, a Ray Kennedy, someone who was supposed to have a higher work rate – then Brooking would be dumped. Kennedy finally declared in a huff that he had not been picked often enough by England and didn't wish to be considered again. That he should have been capped at all is one of the more remarkable aspects of English football history.

Brooking and Keegan grew old, but they did not lose their edge. I remember watching them against Italy at Wembley in 1977. Brooking chipped the laziest of near-post goals, so top-spun, so languid, it barely had the strength to make it. But up rose Keegan, a foot above his taller markers, and headed through the only six inches of air space not covered by Zoff into the top right-hand corner of the net. In the second half the roles were reversed. Keegan slipped his marker with a scurrying, muscular turn; Brooking, as usual, conjured space, and slid the ball home, lazily, falling backwards. I remember his FA Cup-winning goal – a rare header from a mis-hit Stuart Pearson shot – and most clearly of all the goal he himself rates as his best. It was in the Nep Stadium against Hungary: he cut in (if that's not too active a word for Brooking) from the right wing, looked up and uncurled a 35-yard swinging left-footer that lodged with a crunching finality between the far upright and the stanchion. We were impressed, particularly those of us who find it difficult to get the ball airborne at all with the wrong foot. Brooking remarked in his autobiography that he assumed when young that a professional must be equally good with both feet, so he just practised until he was.

In the 1982 World Cup Finals both Keegan and Brooking had been injured, but were fit enough to be considered for the crucial game against Spain, which England needed to win by two clear goals. Neither was selected. Greenwood preferred Tony Woodcock to Keegan and Graham Rix (Rix!) to Brooking. For 70 minutes England panted and sweated, but no one looked likely to sore a goal. With 20 minutes to go, Greenwood brought on Keegan and Brooking. Keegan missed a chance he would have taken if he had been warmed up. My recollection is that Brooking was in possession about eight times. He lost the ball twice in the tackle. Twice he passed it square or just disposed of it. Twice he opened the defence to create respectively England's best and second-best scoring chances of the match. And once he went clean through to see his shot ricochet off the goalkeeper's outstretched body. It was the team's closest effort. If he could do that in 20 minutes, you wondered what he might have done in the course of the match. What successive managers could never swallow was the first statistic – twice losing the ball in the tackle – which, to be fair, was not untypical. Always keeping possession in the tackle is pointless if you cannot then do something with the ball – a fact no England manager, not even Greenwood, has ever really accepted.

Brooking was the most beguiling and most skilful player West Ham have produced in my time. His famous dummy, his ability to lose a man by shrugging his shoulders and shifting his weight, were made more remarkable by the fact that – lovely build apart – there was something essentially quite ungainly about him. But what made his game so ravishing to watch was his ability to make other players look ordinary, or even stupid. This he did with his passing. It might be with one of his characteristic near-post balls, when the big guns were gathered at the other side, but most exquisitely it was with the pass placed casually into no-man's-land. Crowd and defenders would look on for a moment in disbelief. Then suddenly it would dawn. The ball was not rolling into no-man's-land at all, but on to the one diagonal that would take the accelerating striker clean through the previously unbreachable defence.

The West Ham crowd was spoiled by this kind of thing for years. They loved him for it and they applauded every time, but they took it as their due. Such talents, however, as the present West Ham team sadly demonstrates, come only once in a lifetime. I went to Upton Park for Trevor Brooking's final game. It was against Everton whose then newish goalkeeper, Neville Southall, allowed them an improbable 1–0 victory. It didn't spoil the occasion, however. Brooking was called back for a lap of honour after the game, and the crowd gave him as fine a tribute as any man could ask for. In that 10 or 15 minutes of cheering and applause I think they registered their gratitude for the joy he'd brought them over so many winter Saturdays. I have not had the heart to go back to Upton Park since.

But what effect, you ask yourself, did these experiences, these great players and memorable matches have on the impressionable and ambitious young player who watched them? I would like to be able to say that I incorporated this man's strength and that man's skill, Moore's anticipation and Brooking's grace. Like all Sunday footballers, however, I have found it easier to wax eloquent in the changing-room than actually to put into practice any of the things I've seen. I recognized quite early in my football career that I would have to compensate for lack of skill by extra effort. Midfield seemed to me the place where running and tackling could best disguise inadequate ball control and vision. I had played right half at school, so when I took up football again at the age of twenty-two, I had some idea of what was involved. I made my debut for the Guardian Strollers (a team founded by then *Guardian* reporters but now with no links left with Farringdon

Road) in 1977 and have played for them on most Sundays since.

What is the strange compulsion that drags you from a warm bed at nine o'clock on a Sunday morning to stand on a windswept street corner with a kit bag? One year it had something to do with the fact that we were winning our league and playing as well as we could. Most Sundays, though, you do it for the ritual. The arrival at some godforsaken part of London SW38; the long wait for the team kit (why is it always given to the man without a car or a lift? Or, in the old days, to Roger Alton, *The Guardian*'s arts editor, a brilliant right back but a man of pathological lateness?); the biting wind, the bumpy pitch; the feel of the low-grade nylon on your back; the memory of previous weeks not quite expunged from the team socks. The pregame kickabout in which you manage to hit both your shots way over the bar ('two points, Seb'). And then the first long clearance from the opposing goalkeeper which you realize has your name on it. You hope that some gust of wind will take it elsewhere; but no, from a clear sky it homes in on your head, and just in case you thought you could escape, someone calls your name and – ooof. The game has begun. You are awake. In a few minutes you, too, will be shouting at your team-mates as you run down the pitch.

Some years ago we had an infusion of talent in midfield and it was a question of either moving to fullback or not being asked to play so often. I moved to fullback. It's fine, but it means you don't score goals any more. Sometimes I will lumber up into the penalty area for a corner. 'Someone pick up the big man!' 'Get the blond bloke!' It's gratifying to cause some alarm, but in fact I've only ever scored about three goals with my head. My only use is as a diversion. We win as many as we lose these days and after fourteen years' practice I have become a more efficient footballer. Not a good one, but someone you could normally rely on to be in the right place and make a clearance. I have had no real moments of glory. I think the greatest compliment I ever had was paid to me by another long-serving Guardian Stroller, Phil Shaw, now on the sports desk of *The Independent*. We had just won a very competitive cup tie and I had run around a lot in midfield. In the pub afterwards Phil looked into his beer and said: 'Yeah, I used to think you were crap, Seb, but you put the wind up that bloke today.' Not glowing words, exactly, but the best I'm likely to hear. I compare them to those of a reporter shyly quoted by Brooking in his autobiography:

'Brooking simply ignored the mud and gave a performance which had to be seen to be believed.'

I find it harder to get charged up before a game than I did; I don't hate the opposition as much as before, and sometimes even find myself applauding a good save by their 'keeper. All these are danger signs, I know: they mean the boots are, if not hung up, at least halfway to the peg. But I would miss it terribly. The ritual goes on. The silent throwing of the muddied kit into a pile in the middle of the changingroom after defeat; the jolly banter after a win. The grudging icy shower which suddenly flames hot when you least expect it. The stiffening walk to the car, the meditative pint. The postmortem which so often begins: 'We played *all* the football. I just don't understand how. . . .' By the end, you have turned a 1–2 defeat into a huge moral victory. And then – and this perhaps is really why one does it – the afternoon snooze; the sense of selfrighteousness, of exercise properly taken while other people have just sat around indoors.

At this stage there is usually a match on television. I look up from the armchair and see the current West Ham team in action. Julian Dicks is a combative player. Alvin Martin, Tony Gale, they have their points. But why did they let Ince go, I wonder? Why did John Lyall sell so many of his best? Still, you don't stop supporting a team just because they've been relegated. I close my eyes and just hear the background drone of the TV commentary. When the newspaper drops from my hands and I fall asleep at last, it is not the 1990 team that is playing in my head. I am fourteen again and Bobby Moore has collected the ball on the edge of the area. He is moving off in that bandylegged stroll and looking up. Who will he pick out? Hurst has come off his marker. Sissons has room on the left. . . .

Rogan Taylor

Rogan is one of Liverpool's best known supporters but he first adored the Hungarian Puskás and the great Réal Madrid team of the 1950s and 1960s, before he began slumming it at Anfield. After seven years in the Far East he returned to Liverpool to work as a gardener and took a degree in Primitive Religions. After the Heysel tragedy Rogan called for a trade union of fans, and the Football Supporters' Association was born.

Puskás and the Réal Thing

ROGAN TAYLOR

For us it was the end of an era. In play, the Hungarians were so much better that had we lost 14–3 no one could have complained. Puskás mesmerized our defence. Halfway through the first half, one felt physically sick with apprehension.

Hungary had speed, magnificent understanding and they positioned themselves like footballing gods. The game was the most glorious exhibition of sustained brilliance I ever saw. I confess to never having enjoyed football so much – and yet so little! – at one time.

England v Hungary match report, *Liverpool Daily Post*, 26 November 1953

Four of those goals came from outside our penalty area. We should never have lost.

Sir Alf Ramsey in 1966 on the same match

I suppose in 1953 I was the perfect age for adoration – just eight years old. Born in Liverpool, on the edge of what outsiders now call Toxteth but we always knew as the South End, I grew up at the end of a war that had laid waste to much of the city. With bomb sites everywhere, we were never short of somewhere to play football, though close control of the Hungarian kind was somewhat limited by strewn rubble.

By some freakish accident, no one in my family was particularly interested in football. Located on the south side of town, we were far away from Anfield and Goodison, and never witnessed the huge crowds of up to 80,000 of the faithful gathering for their Saturday afternoon rite. The great names and players of Everton and Liverpool were never mentioned at our fireside, and there was no television in the corner to incite an interest. Consequently, as a kid I lost my heart to the game itself, without confusing that affection with a local football club. I fell in love innocently, with only a tennis ball at my feet, and no red or blue shirt in my imagination. It couldn't happen now.

The television coverage of football today reaches youngsters before they can play the game. Their souls are sold direct to sponsors' shirts. The over-televised clubs are known more intimately than the local teams. But at the beginning of 1953 we had no telly and – as far as I knew – neither did anyone else. It took the coronation of Queen Elizabeth II to persuade my folks to get one. Thank God she got crowned that June! Otherwise I would have missed the most memorable televised match of my life: England *v* Hungary at Wembley, a month before Christmas 1953.

It was love at first sight for me. Ferenc Puskás, the pot-bellied inside left with a record that makes Ian Rush look like a park player. He scored 85 goals in 84 internationals for Hungary and 35 in 37 European Cup matches for Réal Madrid. I recently heard a Koppite at Anfield, after a magic run from Barnes, shouting: 'Oh Johnny Barnes, I want to marry him!' That's how I felt about Puskás.

The Hungarians didn't come from beyond the Blue Danube without a reputation. I for one had already heard tell of the 'Magic Magyars'. My best mate – the son of committed communist parents – had been singing their praises ever since the Hungarians had won Olympic Gold in 1952 (as if this somehow reflected well on the Party). So we had already attempted wrapping our tongues around strange names like Czibor (left wing), Boszik (right half) and Hidegkúti (centre forward). And who had ever heard of a first name like Ferenc? We knew the Hungarians were good, but weren't England the best? We had Matthews, fresh from his Wembley triumph with Blackpool the previous season; we had Finney and Stan Mortensen up front; Gil Merrick in goal and Billy Wright running the game at right half. We had never been beaten at home since football was invented. We would soon see how good these 'Continentals' were.

It was billed by the newspapers as the 'world championship' game. Despite being played on a Wednesday afternoon, the match was all-ticket and a complete sell-out. That familiar modern warning, 'fans without tickets are advised not to travel', was announced over and over again. The Hungarian inside right, Kocsis, thought doubtful, was pronounced fit to play but sadly Tom Finney failed a late test and George Robb of Spurs was named for the left wing.

There was much newspaper chat about the renowned lateral passing of the Hungarian team, which involved playing the ball accurately across the line of defenders and awaiting an appropriate opening for a telling through ball. This was a technique opposed to the classic English game of hoofing it up field towards a big centre forward and hoping for the best. Many column inches were spent discussing how England might deal with the superb tactical brain of Hungary's deep-lying centre forward, Hidegkúti. The five previous encounters between the two teams were recalled hopefully, England having won four of them, trouncing Hungary 6–2 at the last meeting in 1936 at Highbury.

The pre-publicity for the match worked a minor miracle at Dovedale Road Junior School which I attended. It was announced on the day before the game that the headmaster – not one famous for an abiding love of football – had granted a holiday to the school for the afternoon of the match. We would all be set free at 2 p.m. in plenty of time to get home and watch (or indeed listen to) it live. The anti-Imperialist parents of my best friend, understandably unmoved by the prospect of the coronation, had refused to buy a television set on cue. My friend and I therefore headed straight for my front room. Our telly had a 9-inch square screen, but with the addition of a huge magnifying glass suspended from its top (I kid you not!) it could be transformed into a magnificent 12 inches. As both teams warmed up before the game, you could see one or two of England's players warily eyeing the quick-fire, short ball passing of the Hungarians. Their powerful shooting at goalkeeper Grosits also provoked a buzz of interest from the Wembley crowd, for the 'Continentals' were supposed to be a bit weak in the shooting department. This particular English myth had grown up in the prewar years, along with the one about how they couldn't get 'stuck in' like us Brits. (The former myth quickly died the death; the latter, inexplicably, still lingers on.)

As captain, Puskás stood in the centre circle, waiting to exchange pennants and flowers (a very suspect 'continental' innovation) with his counterpart, Billy Wright. The niceties over, Puskás nonchalantly juggled the ball from boot to knee, to shoulder and down to thigh. Wright, whose duty it was to mark Puskás that afternoon, looked like he was trying to swallow an orange whole. Within 90 seconds, the Hungarians were one up. It was a gorgeous goal. Centre forward Hidegkúti dummied first one, then a second English defender, drifted right just outside the penalty box, and whacked the ball past Merrick before he could blink. We could hardly believe our eyes. The deep play of Hidegkúti that day was a revelation to us. He was like a combination of Franz Beckenbauer and Marco Van Basten. He covered an enormous amount of ground, from outside his own box, picking up short balls from his defence and laying them off to Puskás or Kocsis, before arriving to score at the other end. Hidegkúti had another goal disallowed in the 8th minute but hit the Hungarians' second after Mortensen had laid on an England equalizer through Jackie Sewell.

The Hungarians' third goal was pure genius. I'll take the memory of it with me to my grave. Superb play by Czibor released the ball to Puskás, positioned at the right-hand corner of the 6-yard box. As Billy Wright's thundering tackle was launched, Puskás dragged the ball back sharply with his left foot, body swerving to the left simultaneously, and smashed the ball into the roof of the net. Wright's tackle seemed to be still in transit as Puskás turned towards the centre circle, arm raised in triumph, walking away. My mate and I were stunned. It was not just the speed and brilliance of the man, *he had dragged the ball back with his studs*. Now, we had seen newsreel clips of the dancing Matthews and the darting Finney before. But we had never seen anyone drag a ball back like that! We both leapt to our feet and my mate took off his school cap and hurled it into the air, crashing it into the light shade. (I remember my ma not appreciating the appropriately revolutionary gesture.) It never occurred to either of us to rue the fact that England were getting stuffed for the first time. It was exhilarating, truly marvellous, sheer joy. Better than sex, drugs and rock 'n' roll would ever be.

By half-time it was 4-2. Wing half Boszik – another wonderful player – had added Hungary's fourth, while Stan Mortensen had pulled one back for England. God knows what manager Walter Winterbottom was advising in the England dressing room during the break. 'Attack boys, attack. It's your only hope!' Whatever it was, England started the second half with Matthews at his best and Grosits forced to a brilliant save. Boszik got the Hungarians' fifth in the 6th minute nevertheless, and Hidegkúti volleyed in the last from a perfect Puskás chip.

Puskás's shooting was ferocious. His left foot needed very little drawback to cannon the ball forward. He took a free kick at one point and poleaxed Billy Wright, a good 12 yards away. The ball rebounded back to him and he promptly poleaxed Alf Ramsey. Puskás was a great dribbler too, with lightening pace and George Best-type inspiration. (How he accomplished all this with a pot belly remains a mystery.) But it was the ball control skills that most amazed us. We had never seen that kind of gifted intimacy with the ball before. Most of us now think of it as archetypically Brazilian. But we first saw it from beyond the Iron Curtain of Eastern Europe.

The headlines in the papers next day made much of the Iron Curtain imagery. 'Curtain down on England supremacy' was typical. But the kids I knew couldn't care less. We had seen the Promised Land (with a vaguely Socialist aura clinging to it) and we set off in imitation. Gone were the English heroes whose identities we automatically assumed with a ball at our feet. No longer 'I'll be Matthews, you be Mortensen'. The playground rang with foreign names – Hidegkúti suffering particularly badly under the Scouse variations. I was a natural inside right, but immediately switched to inside left and tried to develop the stunning left foot shot. The pot belly proved easier. From then on, we looked religiously for Hungary's results in *Charles Buchan's Football Monthly* and thrilled to their 7-1 defeat of England in Budapest a few months later. We followed their progress through the World Cup the next summer and were outraged when West Germany beat them 3-2 in the final, coming back from 2-0 down as well.

The Hungarian revolution in 1956, followed by its brutal suppression, knocked the stuffing out of any hazy ideology still attached to our football. We waited and watched for the talented debris of the Hungarian national side to resurface. Puskás eventually made his way to Spain and joined Réal Madrid in 1957. My support trailed after him and for the next five years I honeymooned with the greatest ever Réal side. They were worthy successors to the Hungarians. In addition to Puskás, there was the genius of Gento and the sparkling Del Sol (what a name!) ; not to mention the incomparable Di Stefano, playing a similar deep game to Hidegkúti's. Of course, I could only follow Réal Madrid from afar. But every newspaper clipping or picture, and every snippet of film that somehow filtered its way through the abiding xenophobia of the English media coverage, was cherished. At any one moment, I could give you chapter and verse of their current league position (most often top), leading scorer (usually Puskás), and whom they would meet in the next round of the European Cup. Their distance from me and the exotic setting (at least as I imagined it) in which they played their football merely enhanced their attraction. I hardly deigned to notice the parochial footballing events on my own doorstep.

The great Manchester United side did strike a chord however, in 1957. Duncan Edwards looked a fantastic player and I held a secret wish that Réal might sign him. I was especially impressed by the fact that United (Busby, of course, the man of vision) took Europe seriously. It seemed hardly credible that the Football League should actually go out of its way to make life difficult for any club seeking to play in European competitions. (It 'interfered with the fixture list' according to the league management.) You would have thought everyone would be falling over themselves to play such great sides as Europe produced. Hadn't we learned anything from the Hungarians' overwhelmingly superior tactical approach and ball skills? Have we ever learned?

Even the terrible tragedy of the Munich air crash in 1958 could not eclipse the Réal side from my mind. I did weep when I heard the news, perhaps particularly because I had just been presented with a complete set of the United team's signatures, collected by the pilot who flew them out to Germany. (He had a girlfriend living in the flat below us.) By the time I received them, they were almost all the signatures of . dead men.

In 1958, Réal won the European Cup for the third year running, beating Inter Milan 3–2. I was ecstatic. They went on, of course, to win it five times on the trot, culminating in that 7–3 victory over Eintracht in Glasgow, 1960. I saw the game in its entirety. It was breathtaking. Puskás hit four goals. The match had an enormous impact in Britain – not unlike England v Hungary in 1953. After the referee blew his final whistle at Hampden, over 30,000 fans refused to leave, standing for over half an hour in reverent awe. For many British viewers, it was little short of a revelation to watch Réal Madrid in full flight. I was quite scathing of course, encountering the sudden converts to this joyous, liquid style of play.

'They've been playing like that for years,' I would say knowledgeably, 'they're the best club team in the world.' But they had to do it here in Britain it seemed, before anyone might concede their superiority. Despite the stunning lesson from Hungary seven years before, 'continental football' had remained for most people an exotic frippery on the margin of the real game (which we played best of course). For me Réal were the real thing.

It was 1962 before my heart finally settled on a team closer to home. Ironically, Réal Madrid lost in the European Cup Final that year, despite a Puskás hat trick. My best friend had become a Stalinist Evertonian but another of my mates dragged me along to Anfield to watch a young side leading the Second Division under a rising new manager, Bill Shankly. Liverpool didn't look too good to me. It all depends on what you're used to, doesn't it? I must admit they have improved since.

In 1966, 80,000 fans turned out at the Bernabeu Stadium in Madrid to honour Ferenc Puskás at his testimonial match. I was there in spirit, one of the no doubt many thousands of his admirers unable to make it for the final embrace. He was a truly great player who set the benchmark for my lifetime's love of football, and elevated it unforgettably into a glorious thing.

Brian Glover

Brian comes from Barnsley, supports Barnsley FC, and drinks, when he can, Barnsley Bitter. After twenty years as a professional wrestler – Leon Arras – he switched to acting via copy writing for the Barnsley Chronicle. *Acting highlights include* Charles the Wrestler *at the RSC,* God *in* The Passion *among many roles at the National Theatre, getting beaten up by John Wayne in* Brannigan, *voicing '2000 perforations let the flavour flood out', in the Tetley tea bag commercial. Television credits include 'Campion' and 'Porridge'. He also writes a weekly column for the* Yorkshire Evening Post.

The Bakehouse and Barnsley

BRIAN GLOVER

That'll be the day that you make me cry

Buddy Holly

'**Y**ou're dropped. Not my decision, tell your dad. Now off you go. Don't forget to tell him. Your dad. Nothing to do with me. Right, you two, hands out! Straight out!' I must have still been standing there. 'Off you go!'

Even out in the corridor I could hear the swish swish of the cane followed by the two involuntary yelps. Then hear him bark out again, 'Other hand! Straight out!' Then again. Swish, yelp! Swish, yelp! I kept thinking, I wish it was the cane that I'd been sent for rather than to be given the news that I'd been dropped from Barnsley Boys. You get over the cane, no bother, but I'd never get over being dropped from Barnsley Boys. I was right, it was 1949, and it still rankles.

In the same year Barnsley Boys defeated Derby Boys in the final of the English Schools Trophy. It was a two-legged affair; we licked 'em 3–1 at Oakwell, and 27,000 witnessed it, then got stuffed 0–1 in the second leg at the Baseball Ground, and 21,000 saw that. Barnsley Boys were, without doubt, the best schoolboy team in the land, and as a reward Barnsley FC had signed on the team, *en bloc*, except for the centre forward who signed for Wednesday in dubious circumstances. Skullduggery was mooted, and not without foundation – an eye-witness had seen a brand new gas cooker being carried into their house from a big van with a Sheffield address on its rear doors.

I'd played in the semi-final against Swansea Boys at Vetch Field. We beat 'em by the only goal of the game, and clinched our place in the final. I played well. Followed instructions. The coach had said: 'That lad there, him in short trousers, see him? He's only thirteen, but he can play, name's Allchurch. Got a brother called Ivor who's a pro; don't let him out of your sight. If necessary, you know what to do.' I'd been in long trousers for two years; I was all over him like a big dog, and I didn't have to resort to sticking in the clog.

Then out of the blue I'm summoned back to my old junior school and delivered this bombshell. We lived down Lundwood, an overspill housing estate just outside Barnsley, but by this time I was a big lad, and going to the grammar school up in town. I was somebody down Lundwood, I went to school on a bus. The reason I'd been summoned back to my old juniors was because the headmaster was on the Barnsley Boys selection committee, and they must have thought it would soften the blow if it came from someone who'd seen me grow up; even got me through the eleven-plus. There was also the consideration that my old junior school headmaster knew my dad, and knew his reputation.

My dad was a wrestler. He wrestled as the Red Devil, and I've often wondered what the neighbours thought when they saw the red, balaclava-like masks bouncing on my mam's washing line on Monday mornings. Even before that he'd been a boxer. He had spent his entire working life in the ring trading blows. He'd well over 100 fights in the 1920s and early 1930s, and two wonderful cauliflower ears to prove that a lot of the punches hadn't missed. It was an era in boxing when there was little or no medical supervision, and although I didn't realize it at the time my dad had had far too many fights and taken far too many punches. As my mam always used to say, 'Your dad just flies off the handle', which was why my old headmaster was so keen to disassociate himself from the decision to drop me.

That my dad was a wrestler was, I suppose, the real reason I followed in his footsteps and spent twenty years of my life bouncing around the pro-wrestling circuit, but being dropped by Barnsley Boys also had a lot to do with my subsequent choice of career. Football boots were very nearly the tools of my trade, not wrestling boots.

I'd been summoned up to my old junior school from out of our back yard. Why I wasn't at school I don't remember, but I wasn't, because I do remember my mam came out into the yard to tell me that Mr Sykes wanted to see me up at the juniors, and that was unusual. My mam usually just stood at the door and screeched my name, and I usually ignored it until the inevitable, 'I'll tell your dad!'. I didn't ignore that. For her to come and fetch me out of the yard she must have known something was afoot.

I used to spend a lot of time in our back yard in football's halcyon days just after the Second World War. Most of the time my only companion was a football. At least that's what folk would have thought if they'd ever bothered to look into our back yard. A lad alone with a ball. How wrong they would have been. I'd a team of mates in the yard with me, and they all played for Barnsley. In goal was Pat Kelly, athletic and unorthodox, the Grobbelaar of his day. In front of him Ernest Swallow and Gordon Pallister; Ernest was clout, and Gordon was class. Right half, the legendary Sid 'Skinner' Normanton. At centre half, Kitchen, motto 'None Shall Pass'. Left half, Arthur Glover, no relation, but if he played well he was my Uncle Arthur. Forward line: right wing, Gavin Smith, who could run so fast that sometimes he couldn't stop and would end up in the crowd with us lot behind the goal; then George Robledo, a Chilean god who, for some unknown reason, came down to earth at Oakwell; centre forward Richardson, inside left, Jimmy Baxter who should have played for Scotland, and last but certainly not least, on the left wing, Johnny Kelly, who did play for Scotland, twice. What a team!

I played with that lot in our back yard. They were on my side. My team. Johnny Kelly would cross the ball from the left, and I would rise like a trout to the fly, a certain goal, but somehow Frank Swift managed to get a fingertip to it, and it was over the bar. George Robledo never missed though, even if Big Swifty was in the net. He scored a lot of goals in our back yard did George Robledo, but it was always me who laid the ball off to him, or nodded it down in the box, so he could bulge the net with one of his blistering drives. Then George would shake my hand in recognition of my contribution to the goal, and we would trot back to the centre spot together. We never cuddled; footballers who had partings didn't cuddle.

Next door's had a bakehouse, at least that's what it was called although I never saw anything baked in it. I used their bakehouse wall to practise my throw-ins. It wasn't easy. There was a high wooden fence separating that wall from our yard, and then a big gap, and if I didn't sling the ball with all my strength it wouldn't bounce back far enough, and it'd drop the wrong side of the fence. Then I'd have to climb over to get it back, and they had a dog, and they didn't call it Leo for nowt. Undeterred, I kept on practising, because as my dad said, you could never be a good wing half if you couldn't throw the ball in. Look at Frank Bokas.

I never saw Bokas – before my time – but my dad said that when he took a throw-in for Barnsley it was like they'd been awarded a corner. Could he throw a ball. According to my dad the only man ever to score direct from a throw-in was Frank Bokas. I don't reckon it's possible within the rules, but my dad always said Bokas had been credited with the goal. It was 22 January 1938, Barnsley v Manchester United, FA Cup, Fourth Round. According to my dad, Bokas threw the ball in, and there was no following wind to help him, but it was heading, like a rocket, straight for the top left-hand corner. If their goalie had had any sense he would have left it alone, but, fatal mistake, he tried to catch it, and fumbled it into his own net. Goal! I often tried to point out that it was technically o.g., but my dad wouldn't have it, and you didn't argue with my dad unless you were daft, because of his tendency to fly off the handle.

There was, however, much more to my continually practising throw-ins against next door's bakehouse wall than just a schoolboy's desire to emulate Frank Bokas. I also had this theory. If I could throw the ball and get it back ten times running without once having to climb that fence and face Leo, then what I wanted to happen would happen. By eight, nine, ten, it was like toothache in my arms, but it was worth it because if I made it, and didn't have to climb the fence, George Robledo would score for Barnsley. It seemed to work.

There had been a time when I used to pray to God for what I wanted to happen. Like if I wanted Robledo to score, or Pat Kelly to save the next penalty he had to face; when I went to bed I would say the Lord's Prayer ten times. The trouble was my dad always told me if you wanted something to happen you had to make it happen by working for it, and the harder you worked the better your chances. God didn't impose any physical effort on my body. I could go straight from 'Our Father' to 'Amen', no bother, just one big breath. One continuous stream of piety. Too easy. Doing the bakehouse wall throw-ins wasn't easy – doing ten knackered me – so to my mind God, as the final arbiter, had been replaced by next door's bakehouse wall. I also knew I was killing two birds with one stone when I did the bakehouse wall throw-ins. At the same time as I was guaranteeing that the headline 'Blades Blunted', or better still 'Owls on Blink' would appear in the

Green 'Un on Saturday night by doing ten bakehouse wall throw-ins, I was also training to be a better wing half.

I soon found that doing ten became easy, and only very rarely did I have to face Leo. I raised my sights and made it twelve bakehouse wall throw-ins for Barnsley to be drawn at home in the next round of the Cup. I made it, and they were. Against Blackpool. I couldn't believe it – Stanley Matthews was to play at Oakwell.

January 1949, Barnsley v Blackpool, FA Cup, Third Round. In those days Blackpool were a power in the land. Not only did they have Matthews, they also had Mortensen, Harry Johnston, and George Farm in goal; they were a team of stars. So much so that it was to be the first all-ticket match at Oakwell, and to get a ticket you had to get up very early on the Wednesday before the game and get in the queue.

We didn't normally have the knocker-up, because my dad wasn't a collier. He had been but he'd soon packed it in as a mug's game, but that Wednesday morning he'd arranged for the knocker-up to call special, as if we were two colliers on days who had to get up at four in the morning. I was already up, dressed, and looking out of the window when the knocker-up arrived with his contraption. It was like a long fishing rod with a reel at the thick end. He turned the reel, and that caused some bobbins to spin round the thin end. He put the bobbins up against your window, and you were knocked up. Colliers always employed the services of a knocker-up, because they said he was more reliable than any alarm clock, and besides he was an old collier who'd been thrown on the scrap heap, and he needed the few bob they gave him at the weekend. My dad gave him half-a-crown for knocking us up just that once.

We walked, silently, in the dark to Oakwell. It was just over two miles, but it didn't seem to take long, even if we didn't talk, and that wasn't through lack of company. There must have been at least 100 of us from Lundwood marching up that road to Barnsley. Men with a mission don't need to talk; they know what they want, and they, and we, wanted a ticket.

When we got there doubt began to raise its ugly head. Perhaps we hadn't got up early enough – you couldn't even see the end of the queue, it just disappeared into the dark somewhere behind Grove Street School. We eventually found it, and joined it. Rumour was rife. Blackpool had been allocated more than their fair share of tickets, because they were First Division. Then we heard that preference was going to be given to ex-servicemen, and that the First World War didn't count. My dad had been at the Battle of the Somme; he always said that was where he got his cauliflower ears – when a couple of Jerry bullets had clipped his lugs on their way past.

Now my dad didn't usually swear in front of me, but suddenly he started, and talking posh. Talking posh and swearing were sure signs he was about to fly off the handle. I told my dad to calm down, he'd no need to worry, I'd done fifteen throw-ins up against the bakehouse wall last night to ensure we got tickets. Fifteen was my world record and virtually impossible, but I'd done it and that was why I hadn't been able to sleep, because my arms ached so much. I don't think he knew what I was on about, but the queue started to move, the moment of crisis passed, and in no time at all we had two tickets.

The following Saturday afternoon Barnsley were out of the Cup. Barnsley 0, Blackpool 1. Matthews slipped it to Mortensen, and he drilled it past Pat Kelly. Even Frank Swift couldn't have saved it. I had known we were doomed the night before. On the Friday night, in order to guarantee Barnsley being in the bag for the draw for the Fourth Round, I had attempted twenty bakehouse wall throw-ins. I failed at eighteen. I almost made it but number eighteen just caught the top of the fence, hung there momentarily, then fell back. I'd hardly strength enough to crawl over that fence to collect my ball. I fell into next door's yard. Even their Leo must have felt sorry for me – all he did was give me a baleful look and a growl, but even a growl from Leo was enough to give me strength to clamber back over our side.

My dad took Barnsley's defeat remarkably well. He even went as far as to agree that George Robledo was beginning to show promise, that he'd looked good against First Division opposition, and he wouldn't be at all surprised if Robledo wasn't on his bike before long. He was right, just a few months later Newcastle were on the phone and Robledo, and brother Ted, flew the nest.

As we walked home from the match my dad mused on things football. How it did you good to be reminded just where you stood in football's pecking order. Johnny Kelly was good, but not good enough to lace Stan Matthew's boots. I pointed out that Kelly had been kicked out of that game by their fullback. My dad conceded that Shimwell was indeed a bit robust. I was surprised at my dad's mild, and reasoned, reaction to the assassination job done on our left winger. Kelly was one of his favourites, and my dad could take grave exception to dirty play. He had been known to fly off the handle when he witnessed clogging.

Like that time when I was playing left half for Lundwood W.M.C. Not that I should have been playing for a Working Men's Club when I was still a schoolboy, but I was good enough, and besides you got ten bob for playing. Lundwood W.M.C. *v* Grimethorpe, it said on the poster, and somebody had written underneath 'Fireworks Assured'. Whoever had written it was right.

Their right winger was an ex-pro, if you can count two guest appearances for Crewe Alexandra as a professional career. Apparently he'd been in the Royal Artillery, stationed at Oswestry, when the clarion call had come from Crewe; it was his moment of glory, something to brag about for the rest of his life. Now he was demobbed, and back down the pit where he belonged. In fact he must have come straight from work because he was still in his pit muck. Mind you, so were some of 'em on our side as well. Ex-pro or not, he must have been either exhausted by his labours down the pit that morning or just well past his sell-by date because I was all over him. He never got a kick, that is until he kicked me. Had I been coming instead of going it would have broken my leg. Then to cap it all, as I was getting up to remonstrate, he back-heeled me in the physog. Cut my eye, loosened a tooth, and left me with a lifelong sinus problem.

I was still spreadeagled on my back when he joined me, the ex-pro, only he landed face down. He didn't get up either. Just lay there making gurgling sounds into the mud, and I could see one white eye flicking in his coal black face. My first thought was that he was having a fit, until, up above, my dad hove into view. Just like a gunfighter blows the smoke from his gun before he twirls it back into his holster, my dad was blowing on his clenched left fist. He was very proud of his left hook was my dad. He'd flown off the handle. Ever after, when I was asked to turn out for a local team, they always added, 'But don't bring your dad.'

Meanwhile back in my old junior school the door of the headmaster's office opened. The two miscreants emerged. One was flapping his hands, arms held out like a scarecrow, the other had his hands tucked firmly into his armpits. The head followed them out. 'Straight back to your classroom.' I was still standing there. 'Tell your dad, you were my choice. Not my decision to drop you.' Then he disappeared back inside his office. The flapping scarecrow wanted to know if it was right that I'd been dropped from Barnsley Boys. I knew then that it would be all over the estate in ten minutes, even if I did ignore the question on the grounds that lads at the grammar didn't answer questions from kids still at the juniors. I wanted to know what they'd done to get the stick. The other one, who by this time had removed one hand from an armpit and was sucking his fingers, managed to inform me, between sucks, that they had been 'Peeing in the inkwells'.

Pondering the indignity of human existence I was sitting on our sofa when my dad made his entrance. 'Is it right?' I confirmed it with a nod. My mam appeared in the doorway behind him. 'Don't fly off the handle, Charlie.' He didn't. He just sat on the sofa beside me, put his arm round my shoulders, and told me it wasn't the end of the world. I told him it was, because Barnsley intended to sign on the team, *en bloc*, if they won, and if I wasn't in the team I would never play for Barnsley. My dad stood up. My mam reminded him again, 'Charlie, don't fly off the handle.' He didn't, he just went upstairs, and then came back down with a pair of his old wrestling boots. 'Try 'em on,' he said. 'Go on, see if they fit.' They did.

Kate Hoey

Tipped to be the first ever female Minister for Sport, Labour's Kate Hoey, MP for Vauxhall, can claim to know a lot more about football than Colin Moynihan. After growing up in Northern Ireland, Kate taught apprentices from the print industry before working as an education officer with young London players. Arsenal are her team, and during her successful by-election campaign a number of the youngsters she had taught were in the team which won the League title.

Arsenal Halt the By-election Campaign

KATE HOEY

Women should be in the kitchen, the discotheque and the boutique but not in football.

Ron Atkinson, 1989

It was a Friday evening. 26 May 1989. I was watching on television the final moments of the Football League season. It was Liverpool *v* Arsenal at Anfield deciding the destiny of the League Championship. Arsenal, who had led the table since Boxing Day, had slipped up during the final week, while Liverpool had won their last ten league matches and the Merseyside Cup Final. The terrible events of Hillsborough appeared to have strengthened their resolve to keep the Championship.

Arsenal needed to win the match by two clear goals. The teams had played 90 minutes. From the Kop came a mixture of whistles and anticipatory celebration. John Barnes and John Aldridge shook hands. The Gunners were only one-up. Then Alan Smith received the ball from defence and played a pass through to an Arsenal player. The player was Michael Thomas. The young midfielder burst into the area. He evaded Steve Nicol and suddenly he was in a one-on-one with Bruce Grobbelaar. The commentator shouted: 'It's up for grabs now.' Michael seemed to linger for an interminable second before chipping the ball into the back of the net to score. At home in front of the television, I celebrated. Arsenal had won the League Championship.

For me that goal will always have an extra importance. I was in the middle of the Vauxhall by-election campaign. The day before I had gone to Arsenal's training ground at London Colney to wish the team well and give Michael a good luck kiss. He in turn, as a voter in Vauxhall, was supporting me in my bid to become a Member of Parliament. Electioneering does not normally stop for anything – certainly

51

not a football match – but I had insisted on being at home to watch the second half. (The ensuing argument about this had provoked the most tense moment of my by-election campaign.)

As I watched Michael's somersault of delight I couldn't help remembering the shy, quiet sixteen-year-old I had first met when he came to Arsenal as an apprentice. At the time I was working with young London footballers, running a 'lifestyle' course. Michael was one of the successful youth team squad in 1983–4. He joined Arsenal at the same time as David Rocastle and as they had known each other on the south London school football circuit, their friendship was natural from the outset. Michael was the youngest of the youth squad, but already the mystique of 'great potential' was attached to him and he had captained the English Schoolboys team.

The youth squad spend two years together, and the first- and second-year apprentices become very close. Now the core of that same successful youth team had come through the ranks and won for Arsenal (and London) their first League Championship since 1971. That the side was so young, and none of the experts had believed they would make it, meant their victory was an especially moving moment for everyone connected with the club. And it was particularly appropriate that Michael, one of the prime examples of manager George Graham's faith in youngsters, should score the winning goal. But it was also the way in which the Liverpool fans accepted their disappointment and applauded Arsenal's lap of honour that made this a particularly proud night for football. To me it was an appropriate end to a very happy time spent in the educational side of football, which had played an important part in my life since I left college. In just over a week I was hoping to be elected to Parliament and if so, my day-to-day involvement with football would finish.

My interest in the game was shaped by my childhood in Northern Ireland with a father who was an avid football follower. Like so many youngsters in those days, Saturday to me was football day. My earliest memories are of being taken to Windsor Park, Belfast. We would get there at least an hour before kick-off and go to the back of the terraces where I would unfold a stool I had brought – a real luxury as I had the back wall to lean against. If we couldn't go to a match – and in rural Ulster it wasn't always possible – the highlight of the day was sitting round the fire and listening to 'Sports Report' on the wireless. There had to be total silence. Not one score could be missed. My father took the football pools very seriously, spending many hours poring over the coupons working on elaborate permutations.

My geography of England was totally shaped by knowing the clubs the Northern Ireland team played for. To this day, Burnley only means Jimmy McIlroy to me, and Luton is Billy Bingham. But in those days it was Manchester United who had my complete devotion. Irish support for Manchester United was very high and I followed the team's fortunes because it was the club of Jacky Blanchflower and Harry Gregg. Then came the Munich air disaster. Just as people seem to remember where they heard about President Kennedy's assassination, I vividly recall the moment when I heard about the plane crash. I had just got off the bus which brought me from my Belfast school. It was late afternoon, and the light was fading fast. My bus stop was at the bottom of a long country road and I would often share the walk home with a neighbour. As a chatty youngster I would engage him in conversation, but this day Frank seemed odd and different. We walked for about five minutes and all my attempts to talk met with silence. Then he suddenly said: 'This is the worst day of my life', and he told me about the crash. The horror of Munich remained with me for many years. I collected every picture – every morsel of information – and made a scrapbook which I have to this day.

My first job in further education was working with young men. I had been given the responsibility for teaching Liberal Studies to the apprentices from the print industry and the London Electricity Board. In those days they were all male, and no one seemed to want to teach them, particularly not the female staff of the college. They were obstreperous and frank about their prejudices. There was just one link that gave me the chance of having a productive relationship with my young trainees and that was my love of football. It wasn't just that I was a fan, but the fact that I knew a lot about the game and that impressed them. From these boys I learnt that you can't expect anyone to respect what you say unless you accord them a similar respect, even if you disagree with their views.

A chance meeting on a train with Bob Kerry, from the education section of the Professional Footballers' Association, led me to work full time in football. We started chatting about my work and Bob told me that all the clubs were meant to give their sixteen- and seventeen-year-olds one day a week release to attend a college course of their choice. Most did, but the lads tended to choose courses with no guidance as to what might be of benefit to them in the future. A boy would enrol for something without any clear motive, maybe turn up for one or two weeks, then, as soon as a chance arose, would miss a week, then another, and then drop out. Very few of the clubs gave back-up support or encouragement, and unofficially some coaches made it clear that in their view the lad would be better off spending an extra day training than wasting time in education. Bob was keen to start a pilot course in London. By the end of the train journey I had been persuaded to meet up with officials from Arsenal and Tottenham.

At Arsenal, Wilf Dixon was my inspiration. He is greatly respected in the football world and had moved from Tottenham with Terry Neill, crossing the north London football divide. He is a believer, like me, that most people are inherently good. He is tight on discipline, but he loves all the lads. 'You have to be able to scold one minute and give them a cuddle the next,' he told me. 'Can you do that?'

The course we devised brought together the young players from Arsenal and Tottenham. Our starting point was to recognize the fact that for these boys football came first in their lives, and there was no point in educationalists saying otherwise. Most of the lads had been dedicated to football from as early as eight or nine. First there had been the hurdle of signing schoolboy forms with a club, then the acceptance at sixteen as an apprentice professional. They all knew the disappointment of friends rejected by the same club. You couldn't tell them they weren't special. To their peer group they were. The Arsenal youth team at that time included Tony Adams, Martin Hayes, Niall Quinn, Gus Caesar, and Rocastle and Thomas.

For sixteen- and seventeen-year-olds, coping with all the normal traumas of adolescence, the added pressure of trying to make the grade in football can be too much. They had only two years to prove themselves and even a minor injury could keep them out of the team for a few weeks. Practice at coping with stress and facing new challenges was therefore built into the course. In the depths of winter we used to go to the Brecons together and survive five days of camping, caving and abseiling off rock faces. Standing on top of a rock face waiting to abseil off was a very frightening experience, and, as Martin Hayes once said: 'There's nothing glamorous about crawling through a cave.'

I also showed them the etiquette of dining in proper restaurants, instructed them how to handle television interviews and, more importantly, I tried to help them realize there is a life outside football – and a life that involves more than just snooker, discos, and watching television.

Even at the top clubs, apprentices do a lot more each week than play soccer, though much of it tends to be football related. They are all expected to perform menial tasks. The boots of the first-team players have to be cleaned, the dressing rooms swept, baths scoured. Each morning at Arsenal it was the apprentices who hauled the kit on and off the team coach at the training ground. In winter it was common to see the lads clearing the pitch of snow so a match could go ahead. Duties are taken very seriously by the staff at Arsenal. Anything not done exactly as Pat Rice, their coach, wants is redone, even if it means boys being brought in specially on a Sunday. Youth matches are played on a Saturday morning, and in the afternoons the apprentices sit together in the Paddock and watch either the first team or the reserves.

Arsenal have a number of their apprentices in digs. Lads from Scotland or Ireland lodge with a second mum – the landlady – and each one is personally vetted by Terry Murphy, the club's youth development officer. Landladies keep in close contact with the club – as 'stay outs' have discovered to their cost. The worst part for the youngster coming to a club isn't the leaving home, however, for most of them are much too excited about going to a 'big club'. But settling in can be hard, and slack time on Sundays can present difficulties. No matter how good landladies are, they cannot replace a family. Homesickness is dealt with in various ways by club coaches. Some believe it's better to be tough and reduce the home visits, while others on the contrary allow extra visits. Remembering my own miserable Sundays when I first came to London, I appreciated what the lads were going through.

Yet their lives are cosseted. Anything difficult is done for them: bank accounts are opened and passports are applied for. There is a myth that all footballers are thick: the truth of the matter is that they don't have to do much for themselves; some clubs do this to mould an acquiescent team. Personally I tried to encourage them to speak out as individuals, and seeing themselves being interviewed on video was a necessary part of that. Many of the apprentices, even before they had made the first team, would find themselves carrying out public duties. Presenting a prize at a youth club or a local school was a regular event. For a lad who had left school himself only months before, this could be a daunting task and one for which we would try to prepare him ade-quately.

The Commons may be the most exclusive club in the world, but some of its members could learn a few things from young footballers about behaviour. No footballer I know would get away with ignoring the ref's whistle in the same way that MPs disregard the Speaker's calls for 'Order'. The House of Commons may have an all-seater arrangement in the style which Lord Justice Taylor is hoping all pro-fessional English grounds will adopt, but there are still vitriolic attacks from The Clock End, and we have had the odd pitch invasion.

There's something special about Arsenal: there is a solidity and cer-tainty about the place. It's not just the famous marble halls that seem to have been there forever, it's the backroom staff as well. When managers change at other clubs the new boss usually brings in his own backroom staff but that hasn't happened at Arsenal. There is a conti-nuity and a family feel around the stadium.

The apprentices I worked with over the years at Arsenal who made the first team achieved something yearned for by millions of young-sters throughout the country. But for Michael Thomas, a twenty-one-year-old from Lambeth whose form had deserted him midway through the season but who kept his cool in the last minute of the last game, it was a moment that changed his life and gave him a special place in football history, and in the affections of Highbury's North Bank who sing: 'There's only one Micky Thomas'. The shirt he wore that night was later auctioned for £10,000.

Michael went on holiday after the Championship triumph, and I went on with my Parliamentary campaign, ably assisted by Niall Quinn, as well as Tottenham's Chris Hughton and his former team-mate, Tony Galvin and others. We held Vauxhall with an increased majority of nearly 10,000. It was quite a time. My only regret is that I was never given the chance to score that winning goal.

Hunter Davies

Hunter goes to White Hart Lane whenever he can, but when things get really dismal he suffers from a bout of Arsenal envy, and rearranges his stamps. A former Sunday Times *journalist, he is now a prodigious freelance writer. He has published a wide range of fiction and non-fiction work, including* The Glory Game *(1972) and* A Good Guide to the Lakes *(1984). He is a former Sunday morning soccer star.*

Selling Spurs Short

HUNTER DAVIES

Marriage has many pains, but celibacy has no pleasures

Dr Johnson

I have been faced with the most awful moral dilemma. Would my conscience allow the obvious decision. Could I ever face my friends. My Saturdays would never be the same again. Oh, how I have agonized as a football fan.

Fans are the only people in football ever troubled with moral or philosophical problems. Most players are mercenaries, they don't give a damn, they have no faith, no loyalty, they will go anywhere, do anything, if the money's right. Look at Mo Johnston. In his confessional, they would have to do extra time.

Look at managers. Swear it's for ever, swear they really care, swear they're doing it for the community, but we all know that, like players, half of them don't know what town they're in. Just feel the wage packet. And directors. Do they care? Do they heck. That bloke who said he'd bought Manchester United. Didn't he try to buy Bolton? Call him a true supporter? They are less faithless than players or managers, but only because they have less opportunity to move around.

You can go anywhere as a fan. No one is paying you. You have signed nothing. You have total free will. Yet in your bones you know you have no choice. You can't change colours, for better or for worse. Your team is your team, till death do you part. It's a very strange relationship which doesn't happen in the real world outside Saturday afternoons.

People who work for Sainsbury's can be head-hunted, just as players or managers in football. The customers of Sainsbury's also move around. They feel no compunction about going for the better attraction, the bigger bargain. So why is it different in football? Why don't fans move around? We're all paying consumers. We all have free choice. Ah, but we don't. We have brainwashed ourselves.

Most football fans, in the first place, get 'chosen', rather than choosing a club. It's our home-town team. Our family always supported it. So it goes. My home-town team is Carlisle United, and I look for their result first, always will do, and watch them when I can. In Scotland I look for Motherwell's result, as my mother came from there and I was taken there as a boy. In 1959 when I first came to London I had no local allegiances. I looked at the map of north London and could have chosen either Spurs or Arsenal. Both seemed handy, but Spurs were doing better, played more attractively, so they became My Team.

Over thirty years I have given them total devotion. I hate Arsenal. Obvious, innit. I'm sick as a frog when Spurs lose and gutted when Arsenal win. I tell people we have two excellent teams in north London. Spurs and Spurs reserves. Ha ha. When someone says they're an Arsenal fan I say, quick as a flash, oh you don't follow football then.

OK, so Arsenal have done better in recent years. OK, so Arsenal have actually won things. I might even admit, forced against the wall, that they have quite a good team at present. So what. Come on you Lillywhites. There is no going back. I made my bed, now support it.

But should I? Spurs don't care about me, why should I care about them? Ah, but it's not a matter of logic. We're into blind faith here. A Spurs supporter supports Spurs. End of story. End of life. I've only got one life. Why should I put up with misery? Why should I not be promiscuous and move around with my favours? I usually take a cold shower when these disgusting thoughts enter my head, but in the last year certain things have dawned on me:

★ I hate the Spurs programme. Yuck. Glossy pix, but appalling prose, aimed at idiots. No wonder football fanzines have taken off. I feel cheated of £1 every time I buy it.

★ I hate the Spurs merchandising. Football appears to have taken a back seat to commerce. Huge inserts in the programme are devoted to selling Spurs kit. Hurry, hurry for a New Spurs Dressing-Room T-shirt, only £8.99, or a New Spurs Suit Carrier, £19.95. I feel sorry for the players, having to pose like dickheads, wearing all that junk. And the parents whose kids want to buy the stuff.

★ I hate the new board. The old directors were pathetic, totally out of touch, but the new board seem only in touch with the sponsors.

★ I hate the executive boxes. If I see another list of their names I'll scream. Yet we're supposed to be grateful to these banks, property companies, hotel groups and international businesses for lashing out their shareholders' dosh.

★   I hate the ticket office. Every season they seem to muck up my tickets, or they get nicked in the post. Order by phone and credit card and they charge you £1 extra. Bloody cheek. The seat tickets anyway are ridiculously expensive.

★   I hate the new press box. It was good in the old days, but now it's so low you can only follow half the match. They obviously preferred to flog off the better positions.

★   I hate Holsten. This is the sponsor. Yes, I know all the clubs have them, but it still upsets me to see their name on the breast of every player. I am a shareholder, and I understand the commercial reasons, but it's the smell which sickens me, the kowtowing for money.

★   I hate not having Hoddle. OK, that is romance for times past. What I mean is that I miss a player whose very presence makes the heart sing, a player whose every move we await with anticipation. I used to go early, when the Blessed Glenn played, just to see him knocking up. Yes, he could disappear in some games, but if he was on the pitch there was always the chance of magic. He alone was worth the admission price.

★   I hate not having Chris Waddle. Another natural, another player it was a pleasure to watch. How can a club like Spurs, with all that money, all that history, have at this moment not one truly exciting player? I have had this out with our esteemed chairman, Mr Scholar, who told me they wanted to keep Waddle, but could not. Once a foreign club sniffs around with £4 million to spend a player gets itchy feet, and that's that. What an indictment. All that sweat to turn our team into an off-shoot of a multi-million-pound sportswear and leisure firm and we're still too small, too poor, to keep our best player happy and at home.

★   I hate Gazza. Why pick on him? Because we're supposed to love him, our only star performer at present. I don't hate Paul Gascoigne as a person of course. It's the Gazza bit that sticks, the creation by the tabloids of this cheeky, chubby little chappie, and all the excuses trotted out for his babyish behaviour.

★   I hate the present team. There, I finally said it. You'll wonder why I never said it first. But all the trivial reasons do matter and annoy me every week. It's also true that if the team were brilliant I would forget all the other complaints.

When Spurs went down in 1977, I did support them, even going to away matches, and there was a great community feeling, as if they somehow did not deserve it. Now, having spent £8 million, who can feel sorry for them? Do I hate Venables? Hard to when he's obviously such a nice bloke, but he has got to do something soon or his days will be numbered.

So what have I done? Don't repeat this, but for the last year I've found myself going to Arsenal when Spurs have been away. What a traitor. What a turncoat. No, hold on. I have been going purely to see them get stuffed. I can get to Arsenal in twenty minutes through back doubles, and the parking is better. Their programme is just as boring but at least it's not a mail order catalogue. They now have executive boxes, but they seem to have put them up with far less fuss and inconvenience. They have the usual awful sponsors, but the place does not reek of new money. The seats are cheaper.

Could I become A Born Again Arsenal Supporter? Blank out the past, forget these thirty years and start again? That would be the logical solution, feeling as I do. It's what my wife recommends. It's only football, she says. People change nationalities, change religions, change wives. Why upset yourself on something so piddling. I think it would take hypnotism to make me sit there and honestly shout for Arsenal.

It's too late. I'm part of that lumpen mass which British football has relied upon for the last 100 years. No other business in the world could possibly get away with it. Treat them like dirt, make them watch in squalor, but they'll still turn up and pay, the poor fools. So far. Note well that Spurs' home crowd has dropped below that of Arsenal. What can I do next? Sometimes I have felt like giving football a break. It could be stamps one of these Saturday afternoons. Nothing too exciting. Nothing too dangerous.

It's now three months since I had those nasty disloyal thoughts. Spurs ended up third in the league. I look back and wonder why it is that with Love, Hatred is not so very far away.

I remember when writing *The Glory Game*, my book on a year with Spurs in the early 1970s, talking to Morris Keston, a lifelong loony

Spurs fan. He never watched the last 15 minutes of any game. It was all too unbearable. Even when they were winning, he knew it might well end in tears. His Love for Spurs was Agony.

Once you're part of the football family, then Love is taken for granted. You are allowed to criticize, as in any family, which is some- thing the club's programme has never understood. Naturally, if an outsider dares to criticize, then that's out of order. But among our- selves, we are allowed to boo, hiss, mock, jeer and scream inwardly when Gazza once again does his silly boy act.

In calm moments, I know only too well that nothing I can think, or nothing the most abusive supporter can shout on the terraces, or the nastiest stirrer write in the Spurs fanzine, or the directors mutter into their whiskies, will ever equal the pain and despair which the players themselves suffer. They know and feel the agony better than we do and have to live with it, seven days a week. We can go home on a Saturday, kick the telly, switch on the wife, and settle down with a Holsten Pils, be sick, and get it over with for another week. They can't escape.

I don't know Terry Venables but I know without knowing him that he knows the worst – and long before we do. He is watching those dummies he bought, day after day. He sees the loss of form before we do. He knows of injuries we'll never hear about. He knows the idiots who will never improve, the ones with domestic daftness buggering up their lives. The ones on drink or dope. The ones who can't be told, the ones too thick to learn. The cowards and the cheaters. I should think in any one month he feels more Hatred for his players than we do in a lifetime. And also Love. So, should we have more pity on the suck- ers? Do they not bleed when we carp and criticize? Of course they do. And they hate us for hating them, thinking as loyal supporters our duty is to offer blind, unswerving support. Hard cheddar. We fans do not pay our hard-earned money to be kind, to contemplate politely in the calm moments, to consider carefully the feelings of the players and the manager. They have chosen to be up there. No one forced them.

And they get quite well rewarded. They must be prepared to be shot at, like politicians, rock stars, writers. Dear God, you should see the horrible reviews I've had over the years for my various books and programmes.

Now, in a calmer mood, I know I can never escape from Spurs. I am caught, as we all are. That's me, and Spurs, for ever. Okay, I won't say it or try to explain it again. You know it makes no sense.

I do not hate Gazza. I take that back. In the World Cup in Italy he looked one of England's best players, which wasn't saying much. He has one enormous attribute which is rare in footballers, in fact rare in most of us. GAZZA HAS TOTAL CONFIDENCE. I like that. I admire that. I envy that. He always believes he can do certain things, even when it becomes obvious he can't. Yet it is clear why Robson refused for so long to stick him firmly in an England team. It's nothing to do with his age, lack of maturity, being silly, losing his head, arguing with the ref, committing petty fouls, all of which are true. He wasn't good enough.

Last season, I never saw him play a really great game for Spurs. Not over 90 minutes. In my mind, he is for ever deep in his own half holding off three opponents with his bum, fighting to make space, doing clever little things, moving sideways, managing to hold on for a bit, then wham, he's on the floor. The ball has gone, and usually his temper. On the other hand, I can remember some smart wiggles, some successful twiddles, some good free kicks, one or two dashes into the danger areas, even the odd goal. That's if I concentrate and think hard, contemplating in tranquillity, then I might conjure up a few of his rare moments of poetry. Mostly, however, I see him messing about, in really stupid positions, making time and space for himself when there's no need, when an easy pass would do, so that he gets caught and gives away a goal, or a dangerous free kick, as he will retaliate for his own mistakes by lunging into some passing opponent, or even breaking his arm on their head. You would never see Lineker do that. In a way Gazza's enormous confidence can be a handicap to the team. They are aware of this confidence, and his innate skills, and are often dominated by his presence, organizing their own play round him, directing themselves to him. Look how often there have been mix-ups in midfield, with Samways and Allen and Howells getting in each other's way, trying to get the ball to Gascoigne, or being mentally browbeaten by his presence when they can just as well be positive themselves. However, as the season ended, Gazza began to emerge as a 90-minute player. Is the best about to come?

I like Lineker. He was never truly a world-class player. His 1986 World Cup glory was luck and a good run, both deserved, but he does have a marvellous temperament. Without his goals last season we might have gone down. I only wish he had that deep-down Gazza confidence. Watch him cry to the heavens, berating himself when he's missed a chance, half apologetic, half pleading. Class players never show that. They *know* they're good and will do it properly next time. Apart from Lineker, who is there, which current players make the heart grow fonder, the blood run stronger? Long pause there. So we'll start a new paragraph.

Eric the Viking, he does quite well in goal, but he doesn't convince. I have to turn away when Van den Hauwe gets the ball; as if we haven't got enough heavies and lumpen proles. By comparison, Fenwick is the master of finesse. Mabbutt – well every team needs a Mabbutt, and Spurs still do, only a better Mabbutt, a really dominant Mabbutt, playing further up, a Blanchflower or Mackay or Souness version, someone to take over the game and inspire the team, especially when things are going badly. I like Mitchell Thomas. I blame Venables for not getting the best out of him. That's his job. What else does a manager do. Having almost chucked him out, he now loves him, but he sits uneasily in the team. Not as uneasily as Paul Allen. He still buzzes around like a stranger at a party, as though no one has introduced him to anyone. Over here Paul, settle down for a moment, I'd like you to meet these chaps, they all play for Spurs, perhaps you've heard of some of them. I like Samways, but I sense he will move on, part of that long line of talented but feeble players, not strong or forceful enough to establish themselves, the sort which Spurs breed then sell on to so-called lesser clubs, like Norwich, where they suddenly harden and blossom. Why can't Spurs do that? Are they overawed at White Hart Lane? Is it the Gazza factor?

Paul Stewart. Hmm. Everybody's fall guy, apart from those who enjoy booing Fenwick. He will, given half a chance and a halfwitted defence, always barge a few goals, but his natural home is the Second Division. That goes for the majority of the present team. Yes, I'm still sitting calmly, and feeling well pleased that they did quite well last season.

The trouble is, I've waited almost thirty years now for another team capable of taking the First Division. Bloody hell, it is Spurs I'm twitting on about, not Carlisle United; one of the all-time great clubs, upon whom enormous north London love and several fortunes have been spent. If they had just one STAR who made my pulse run, who was a pleasure to watch even in the knockabout, then I might be more forgiving. As it is, I have to face facts. I know, as we all well know, that they have neither enough truly talented individuals nor shaped what they have got into a formidable fighting unit.

But, hope springs, love will last, hatreds will come and go, and Spurs will travel on. As we all will, following them into the 1990s. Good luck. And thanks. For the memories, if little else.

Parts of this article first appeared in The Independent *newspaper.*

John Duncan

John has his grandfather to thank, or blame, for taking him to Everton v Wolves in 1977. Despite being an Evertonian for evermore thereafter, his most memorable match is Liverpool 0, Arsenal 2, 1989 ('Laugh? Me?'). Two years before that he became involved in the fanzine When Saturday Comes, *which has established itself as the leader of the new wave of football magazines. From 1984 to 1987 he played at all levels of the London School of Economics teams, and took a degree. In 1978, he organised and starred in a 5–1 victory over a local school team, recalled for his finest moment in football, a diving header from the penalty spot that hit the crossbar.*

Blues Anonymous

JOHN DUNCAN

'One does not love a place the less for having suffered in it.'

Jane Austen

I remember the first game. It was a spiteful, windy day and I was staying at my grandad's. I knew that football existed and that it was important to my elder relations (I was about ten), but like sex I didn't at that time actually know anything about it. Thanks to my grandad I was fortunate enough to find football a few years before I really discovered girls.

A September day in 1977 my grandad took me across a bleak old cemetery from his house in Walton, on Merseyside, to Goodison Park. I remember wondering how many people must have died to fill those graves, and that logically at some point in the distant future the entire world would be one big graveyard. I was as far from being pre-occupied or obsessed with football as you could imagine. Halfway through the graveyard I could hear in the distance the sound of a distorted record and occasional cheers and singing. I knew that this was something to do with football because I had occasionally watched 'Match of the Day' from behind the bannisters at home (a first-class introduction to perimeter fencing) when I was supposed to be in bed. Actually I only did it to see Starsky and Hutch but if I was still awake and undiscovered by the time David Soul caught the baddie and got the girl then I'd usually hang around for Jimmy Hill.

My dad was a rugger and cricket man and my mum was the only girl among three brothers and had an aversion to the game. If it hadn't been for my grandad, I might be spending my Saturdays birdwatching or learning foreign languages. The game my grandad chose for my induction was Everton *v* Wolves. I still have the match ticket stub (row S, seat 78); I can't remember anything about the game itself, but I can still see the pitch in my mind. I had never seen anything so green in all my life and when I walked up into the main stand at Goodison

Park where my grandad had a season ticket, my feet went tingly. It was so huge! Having been brought up in a village outside Leeds and then moved to Harrogate I was unprepared for anything on this scale. I had never seen so many people in one place before, and I had certainly never heard so many people singing together at once.

There wasn't even a church organ at our Catholic services and we had to share a church with the Protestants, which always made me imagine two different Gods passing each other through the roof, and perhaps exchanging pleasantries. Later it was explained to me that even if my fantasy were possible the two Gods would kick the living daylights out of each other, as one would be supporting Liverpool and the other Everton. This was instrumental in converting me to atheism. If God supported Liverpool (which did seem possible at the time) then I didn't want to go to heaven and have him laugh as he told me how he made Clive Thomas think he saw Bryan Hamilton handle the ball. If God supported Everton then how could he allow us to suffer? And why, if he was prepared to send his only son to help the Israelites, did he only bother to send us Gordon Lee?

And now 30,000 people were cheering and clapping as the theme from 'Z Cars' screamed out of the tannoy. It was all a bit much for a boy of ten. Looking beside me to my grandad it seemed as if it might be too much for him. He had a huge smile on his face and was cheering wildly as the teams came on. That first game ended 0-0, and wasn't a very interesting contest. But, I have followed Everton with varying degrees of enthusiasm ever since. Perhaps enthusiasm is the wrong word. Where most people choose their leisure time according to what gives them the greatest satisfaction and enjoyment, following football, of course, just isn't that simple. Only one team wins the League, another a cup or two, and the rest are left to gather the crumbs of delight of occasional victories over rivals. Not only that, going to football in the early 1980s wasn't comfortable or particularly relaxing.

So why go to football? Perhaps because football, like national service, is a good thing because you don't enjoy it. Life is too easy. You can't reminisce about comfort. You can't craft an identity based on luxurious enjoyment of something nice (well not in the early 1980s anyway). Football fans are as nostalgic for moments of despair as much as ecstacy. I can remember one Colchester fan coming into the bar at Leyton Orient after his team had been thrashed 8-0 with a huge grin on his face. He had been there. He had been part of it. He had loved it. For me, and I suspect others, simply winning was never the point. Moaning in unison with thousands of others and sharing their misery is uniquely gratifying in a sanitised, irradiated and pre-packed society. So armed by my grandad with a healthy pessimism and a keen sense of past glories I became a football supporter. It was just as well that I did. Our family has been Everton since the turn of the century, and there is a particular place in the Park End that my great grandfather used to occupy, easily identifiable by a pile of thick pipe smoke which would rise from a spot that he refused to move from his whole life. My grandad was formerly a cobbler and invented a type of shin pad which the Everton players apparently tried out once. When he is drunk (an all too rare event) he can make it sound as if his shin pads practically made Dixie Dean the player he was. On most occasions I am usually drunk enough to believe him.

But living so far away in Leeds was a real problem for a young kid of eleven or so and I was never really able to go regularly until a few years later. I followed them statistically almost from the first, charting the mediocrity of the Gordon Lee years in a scrapbook that contains all the teams and several newspaper clippings from the season that I first went, until it all became too much of an effort. This was bad timing of the first order. For my sins I now possess a complete chronicle of some of the most dismal years in the history of Everton Football Club. As soon as I stopped charting their exploits the team decided to do something worth recording. The last fateful entry is a 1–1 draw with Manchester United in 1982.

The book is punctuated by stickers, which I was never really obsessed with in the way that others at school were (however I did once collect a whole set of dinosaur stickers and a few bubble gum cards . . . my mum would probably put it all down to good potty training). In particular, the club badges that Mobil gave away in the late 1970s brightened up the page if there wasn't a match report. Getting those particular stickers involved going shopping with my mum and convincing her to stop at a Mobil garage, which perhaps shows that the people who come up with these ridiculous things to give away may be on to something after all. Perhaps kids nowadays really do pester their mums for bath towels, mugs and frying pans.

My devotion was hardened by the fact that my best friend at school was a Liverpool fan who never went to games either. We had endless rows about whether or not the other was a real supporter, and about things that neither of us really had any knowledge of (another excellent preparation for adulthood). The thing that cemented our friendship was the pleasure derived from ganging up on the kids who supported Leeds United, one of whom thought Ray Hankin should play for England. I think he is a bank manager now. Serves him right.

As a child living in Leeds during the Revie years, I soon realized that football is about omens as much as skill. I always believed that the result of any game that I did not attend was dependent on something that I either did or did not do. I once got expelled from a PE lesson at school for wearing a full replica kit and a scarf on the day of the Merseyside derby. Fortunately Everton lost, or I would have felt compelled to get expelled from PE each time there was an important game to ensure their continuing success. One of my relatives, naturally a very keen Evertonian, believes his attendance is unlucky after he went to only one game in a season and they lost 6-2 at Manchester United to end a long unbeaten sequence. He reluctantly accepts that he can never go again.

Another lucky ritual I had was to stand at home and listen to the radio while throwing a ball against my bedroom wall and diving to catch it just like my hero George Wood (just like George, I constantly dropped the ball). The theory was that while I continued to catch the ball and make glorious full-length saves across my duvet, Everton could not lose. As my room was right above my mum's, midweek games inevitably meant a family conflict, and at a time when there was already a fair bit of trouble associated with the game my mum and I came very close to football related-violence on a few occasions, though to be fair she did pick me up from Elland Road once after a semi-final replay against West Ham, which we lost.

Apart from Everton being at their tedious worst, that game sticks in the mind as one of those occasions when I was noticed by the players. Having turned up early (my journalist uncle had got me a ticket for the press box and I was definitely the only person under fourteen in there) I had also prepared a banner out of a sheet that I didn't think my mum would miss. Dixie Dean had just died and my banner said 'Do it for Dixie', and I held it aloft in the empty stand as Mike Lyons inspected the pitch before the match. Several of the players pointed up at me and waved and I felt that I was practically a friend of the team. Until I looked up and saw the banner was upside down. I had managed to blow my moment of glory in almost as embarrassing a way as the team did by allowing Frank Lampard to score a late winner with his head.

I was still restricted to occasional visits with my grandad on my increasingly regular family journeys across the Pennines, which magically coincided with Blues' home games. One time I went to see Everton at home to Leeds and to save money took a Leeds supporters' club bus. It was an adventure for the three of us who went (the 'Ray Hankin for England' fan, and another school friend), none of whom had ever been to an away game before. We went in the seats thinking it would be safer, and everything seemed to be going okay when Everton scored early on. Then disaster, Leeds equalized, one of my companions forgot he wasn't at Elland Road and started jumping up and down a lot. Within five minutes I became aware that all the seats that had been empty around us had filled up with menacing-looking young lads. Time to leave. We made a dash for the exit pursued by about ten of these lads and fortunately found a police horse. Most of them stopped chasing and went back. But the nice policeman wouldn't escort us back to our coach and one or two of the ugliest pursuers were still around. As we got out of sight of the policeman one of them charged up to my friend. But before he could get in a kick or punch my mate fell to the ground, rolled up in a ball and started screaming in pain. This so disconcerted the attacker that he ran off. We made it back to the coach and found Leeds had scored a late winner. It was the only time I was glad to have left early and missed a goal.

Finally I became old enough and daft enough to go regularly on my own. Well, nearly on my own. I saw an advert. in the matchday programme for a lift to home games for anyone in the north-east and Yorkshire. I wrote back in my best handwriting and got a call from a gruff Geordie called Michael. They had a space in their minibus and could pick me up on the A1 at Wetherby.

I hope my mum isn't reading this because I have never dared to tell her, but the only way I could pay for that journey was to go without food and save my dinner money at school. This self-deprivation and some collecting of pocket money from my dad meant I could just about afford to go to Liverpool every other week. My mum's fears for my safety weren't made any smaller by the unfortunate fact that my lift was driven by a guy whom she explained worriedly had exactly the same name as some notorious murderer who got hanged. I wouldn't have cared if Charles Manson had been driving, I was going. I was a real fan now, and that was it.

My introduction to regular football-going was also an introduction to a different way of life. Having attended Leeds Grammar School and lived on the outskirts of Leeds, it would be safe to describe my early years as sheltered. Football changed all that. For one thing I discovered, to my surprise, the pleasure that some grown men derive from farting in confined spaces. About ten of us used to cram into a minibus, filled full of all the things that my parents had guarded me from – tabloid newspapers, Embassy Regals, lager and the stench of beer.

Once, while waiting in Wetherby for them to arrive, a girl who was even younger than my own fifteen tender years came over and told me that her friend fancied me. She pointed to a scrawny thirteen-year-old standing timidly by the bus station. It didn't do my ego any harm, but strangely I didn't feel I could turn up the chance of a 150-mile journey with nine Geordies for a bit of innocent snogging. That was how much I supported the Toffees. Later I wished passionately that I had, because we got beaten by Manchester City.

Being a young lad I couldn't go into the pubs with the others, and as the minibus arrived in Liverpool at about 1.30 p.m. for precisely that purpose I was left with a long time to wait around Goodison Park. I passed the time by developing a cherished routine. Chips (I needed them after bunking school dinners all week), and then off to the car park behind the away end to seek players' autographs. Almost all my programmes from this era have totally incomprehensible scrawls on them, as if ten people had tried out their biros. A quick glance at the old programmes makes it look as if a chap called Mark Lemon once played for Everton, or perhaps I went through a completist phase of getting coach drivers as well. Several players obviously tried to show off and sign their names in Mandarin. But it passed the time and was probably as much a ritual for the players as it was for me. I consoled myself that they would miss me if I wasn't there. Occasionally I would try to make an encouraging comment and like to think they heard and appreciated. Like most middle-class boys I had an inflated sense of my own importance, a quality that has unfortunately stood the test of time. This sense was reinforced when I had a long conversation with Mike Brearley at the Harrogate Hi-Fi show about whether or not Geoff Miller should play for England. I didn't really care about Miller (I thought and still think he was useless) but I felt I had to say something and so to seem knowledgeable I argued that if the selectors were going to pick him he should at least be given a few overs and the chance to prove himself. Sure enough next game Miller had several long spells, and unsurprisingly didn't do anything of note. I swore that I could see Brearley thinking what an idiot he was to listen to that arrogant little squirt in Harrogate at the weekend.

In order to make the financial side of being a real hard-core fan at the age of fifteen a little less burdensome, I became a lottery agent. I thought it would be quite good fun and help me to get a free ticket once in a while, as well as being useful to the club and earning me a generous commission. Unfortunately I always made a loss because I felt guilty if I had any tickets left at the end of the week, which meant that I invariably ended up buying any remaining tickets myself just to avoid the embarrassment of having let the club down. It eventually became impossible to sell any at all, after about ten weeks in which no one that I sold a ticket to won a single penny. By now I was having to contemplate cutting out school lunches completely and not even having a Mars bar at break. Things were getting serious.

Things were even worse for the club. Howard Kendall was buying dross like Mickey Thomas, Alan Ainscow, and (oh my God it's all coming back) Alan Biley. I can't remember the last game I went to with the boys from the north-east, but somehow I just stopped. My grandad (noticing that I had got a lot thinner) had tried to convince me not to bother by telling me that true fans stayed away when teams were playing crap, the theory being that the loonies who would turn up if Everton put out a team of doped-up dromedaries enabled the club to keep sending them out and still make money. Eventually I succumbed to his logic.

I reverted to occasional attendance, but never lost interest completely. I remember exactly where I was – gutting an old electrician's workshop – when Adrian Heath latched on to Kevin Brock's back pass, and I went to Wembley in 1984 for the FA Cup win over Watford.

Then I found myself at college in London, ironically within easy access of more Everton games than ever before. My enthusiasm returned and I went to see them whenever they came to town. What an experience. Invincible at Goodison Park they often seemed frail away from home and positively comatose in London. The best moment was undoubtedly the Wayne Clarke goal at Arsenal that effectively sealed the 1987 Championship. That season they lost at Spurs, Charlton, West Ham and Watford, and drew at Oxford. But at Arsenal in March they redeemed themselves when, as two fat Scots-men leaned on my back for 90 minutes and farted copiously, John Lukic passed straight to Clarke who curled the ball back into an empty net. As the Evertonians celebrated I lost my glasses in the crush and the two Scotsmen personally parted the crowd so that no one would tread on them, which goes to show that you should never judge people by the output of their bowels. Liverpool meanwhile were losing at home to Wimbledon. Oh joy! The following week saw Everton at Chelsea. It poured with rain, I ruined two newspapers by using them as rain hats and went home with the back page of the *Kilburn Times* imprinted on my forehead and Alan Harper's 30-yard match-winning drive imprinted in my mind.

I didn't attend the European Cup Winners' Cup Final against Rapid Vienna in Rotterdam, 1985, because my wise grandad, two weeks before Heysel, convinced me there were rumours that there was going to be trouble. As it was I spent the night in a college bar, and accidentally smashed my watch in a moment of drunken ecstasy when Andy Gray scored in the first half. It was about 30 seconds before I looked up at the TV to find that it had been mysteriously dis-allowed. After Everton's eventual 3–1 win I went home with a traffic cone on my head telling jokes to people on the tube. I hugged every-one I could find and fell asleep happy.

Being banished to London, as I now am, is genuine torture. Watch-ing Everton away all the time is as near to hell as you can get. Their inability to resist back passing and a recent addiction to offside traps make the scarcity of opportunities to watch them less of a strain. There's no escaping it, I'm a part-timer now, my support cut to occasional, frustrating afternoons with other hordes of exiled Evertonians bemoaning their style of play in miserable away ends in the capital. Still it's too late to give it up. Following Everton is like having a chronic drink problem. But as any reformed alcoholic will tell, you never really stop being one, however long you have stayed away. So as they say at Blues Anonymous, my name is John and I'm an Evertonian.

John Tummon

John was born and brought up in Wolverhampton. He moved to London where he took a degree in history and achieved his most memorable moment in football: accidentally leading a group of Wolves supporters into the Tottenham fans' end at White Hart Lane. A natural Wanderer, he has had a series of jobs from busking to teaching, and now works as a community relations officer in Manchester, from where he travels faithfully to Molineux. He is a contributor to the fanzine, Rodney Rodney.

The Resurrection of Wolves

JOHN TUMMON

Businessmen they drink my wine,
Ploughmen dig my earth,
None of them along the line,
Know any of its worth.

'All Along the Watch Tower', Bob Dylan

Forget President Kennedy's assassination – most Wolves fans can still tell you exactly what we were doing on 2 July 1982 in that chilling moment when we heard the news that Wolverhampton Wanderers Football Club had folded. There was no precedent, no rumours and no real warning signs; the news came straight from Hell, like the unexpected death of a healthy friend.

It came out of my television as I was cooking in our Manchester kitchen, sucking me through the open doorway into the living room to stand transfixed and terrorized while shots of the club offices were panned up on the screen. My ears took in the newsreader's words but the rest of me didn't want to believe it. The news tailed off into a hastily assembled obituary about Wolves's achievements down the years. I went back into the kitchen and cooked the rest of the meal on automatic pilot. Brain and soul were elsewhere, coping with the sudden onset of grief, registering fond memories, re-visiting promotion celebrations, League Cup victories and all those daft, crazy times in the life of a football fan. Each flashback was cut off from the rest by a jolting realization that Wolves were dead and that a part of me would die as a result.

Wolverhampton and the Black Country is football country. South Wales has rugby union; Lancashire and Yorkshire are rugby league strongholds outside of and between Liverpool, Manchester, Sheffield and Leeds. Only the area between the Tyne and the Wear shares the same cultural dependence on football as the source of local pride and identity, alongside making things. It was the football club's international achievements in the 1950s which put Wolverhampton on the map. Who has ever heard of Dudley, a few miles south of Wolverhampton and almost as big? Dudley is like Salford – a name on a motorway sign which means nothing to people outside the immediate area. Football clubs like Wolves, Sunderland and Burnley have at times not only been the main but the only way in which the people of the respective communities express who they are. To illustrate this, some years after the dreadful day in 1982 the 1987–8 Sherpa Van Trophy was held – a knockout competition for Third and Fourth Division teams with a Wembley final at stake. Two of these three clubs, Wolves and Burnley, made it. What had been seen as a bit of a joke cup final drew a crowd of 81,000 – without any neutrals and hangers-on who used to fill Wembley to its old 100,000 capacity in the days before the right to stand was done away with. Wolves took 50,000 supporters down to London that day, probably the largest number of supporters of one club to watch its team away from home since Manchester United won the European Cup in 1968. That is just under one in five of the total population of Wolverhampton. That is what football means, and what Wolves mean to the town. Yet in 1982, as the rest of the country gawped at the World Cup on television, a football town was in mourning for its club.

Allegiance is a powerful thing, especially when it dates back to our earliest years. If it takes hold in childhood, when we feel and express our emotions more vividly and with less inhibition than later on, we can never, ever shake it off. Wolves took hold of me just after I jilted Father Christmas – in the mid-1950s. For the next few years they occupied much the same sort of place in my life as had dear old Santa before I sussed him out: a source of fantastic memories tinged with magic. My favourite one was about how England had lost at home for the first time ever, 6–3 against Hungary, a country a long way away to the East. Everyone in our country was very unhappy about this, and even more so after the Hungarians beat England 7–1 in Budapest a short while later. Wolves, the champions of England, bravely challenged Honved, the champions of Hungary. Honved accepted and fielded five of the internationals who had thrashed England, but Wolves beat them 3–2 in front of 55,000 people at Molineux and everybody in the country was happy again. I was even happier when Wolves took on Réal Madrid in 1957, at the height of the Spaniards' success, drew 2–2 in the Bernabeu Stadium and won 3–2 in Wolverhampton. The next day the newspapers declared that Wolves were the champions of the world.

And so it was that a little boy was growing up taking it for granted that his local club were only a little lower than the angels in the scheme of things; a sort of fixed star around which other clubs revolved with enormous respect. What chance did I stand? I never knew a time before Wolves were the champions of the world, the galaxy, and the known universe. I presumed it had always been like that and would always remain so. When I invested my emotions in Wolverhampton Wanderers Football Club I thought I was on to a certain thing: nobody told me they sometimes didn't win. When I found out I cried my little eyes out.

By 1982 I had learned not to cry about football, but when Wolves went under I was inconsolable, just like that little boy from a generation before after Danny Blanchflower's Spurs came to Molineux and won 4–0.

During many of the seasons in between, the Molineux loudspeaker system always heralded the game with music called 'The Liquidator', a stirring ska instrumental by Harry J and The All Stars, to which we used to clap our hands and stamp our feet on the wooden terraces of the North Bank. The acoustics of the North Bank are forbidden fruit now and have been these past five years, but the liquidator has visited us twice: his first coming in 1982 was as the Grim Reaper, his second in 1986 as the avenging Angel delivering us from four years of systematic asset-stripping under the regime of the mysterious brothers Bhatti.

Relegation is one thing – as a fan you can see what is going on on the pitch, but the boardroom remains hidden from view, apart from the occasional leak in the press. This reminds us of our place and that the clubs we call ours are not really ours at all but the personal fiefdoms of individuals like Harry Marshall, who resigned as Wolves' chairman in June 1982, to make way for the two-week interregnum of Doug Ellis in between his two stints at the Villa. Think about it – to most football people Ellis is synonymous with Aston Villa, and yet there he was, moving in to Molineux. How many Villa fans on the Holte End have given up their allegiance to Mr Ellis's club and come over to Wolves?

'Our' clubs are in the hands of businessmen and almost entirely at their mercy. They are legally entitled to do anything with their property, including changing it into something entirely different.

In 1982 we had an early and near fatal encounter with the predatory men who have moved into football. The Bhatti years of 1982–6 were quite unlike anything which supporters of a big club expect to go through. Wolves lost virtually everything – money, property, players, facilities, and the respect of the rest of the football fraternity. As the club became a laughing stock the local economy was also having its heart ripped out as one factory after another was closed down in an area that for 100 years had been the workshop of the Empire. Suicide rates began to rise, and it seemed for a while as if every time I returned home from Manchester somebody else I knew had been made redundant.

The brothers Bhatti, purveyors of bouncy cheques and promisory notes, conned their way into the club in 1982 under cover of one of its greatest heroes, Derek Dougan, at a time when Wolves were desperate for a saviour – even Bhattman – and left it in 1986 unable to pay the milkman. In those pre-fanzine, pre-Football Supporters' Association days speculators could be speculators and football fans were lowly serfs hoping for a gallant knight to happen by.

He did of course: at exactly three minutes before the receiver's deadline, Dougan reappeared, living proof of the club motto, 'Out of Darkness Cometh Light'. We were so mesmerized by this second coming, that it was nigh on two years before any of us identified Bhattman as the blur riding side-saddle on the Doug's white charger. Dougan's first coming had been scarcely less dramatic – a home debut hat trick against Hull City – but this time he announced his intention to 'give Wolves back to the supporters' at the first public meeting of the new company. He even stood on the terraces for the first match of the season.

Everything seemed to gel. The receivership was, after all, no more than a blip, and it had served to give us the rare privilege of having one of our own heroes as chairman and chief executive. The team rounded off the born-again atmosphere: apart from John Burridge, 'Zico' Palmer, Andy Gray and Kenny Hibbitt, it featured local youngsters Mel Eves and Wayne Clarke up front. We swept to the top of the Second Division on a wave of emotion, and at the beginning of the New

Year, we beat Leeds to go 14 points clear. It seemed all over bar the shouting, but in fact the shouting was all over too – that Leeds game turned out to be the last time a Wolves team played a good game of football for over four years. Although we scraped promotion to the First Division, celebrations were muted because we all knew the team needed strengthening.

Bhattman's asset-stripping began in earnest two months into the following season with the sale of the most saleable commodity on the club's books: Andy Gray, the Scottish international, personality and goalscorer whom John Barnwell had signed on the Molineux pitch for £1,469,000, a British record fee at the time. But the Bhattis wanted quick bucks and sold him to Everton for one sixth of that.

The rot set in, with the first of many 'worst ever' runs, although at this stage good young players still considered Wolves a great club and wanted to come. Sammy Troughton was the pick of these – a young Irish midfielder with poise, a good touch and vision, he looked set to become Bhattman's Bhoy Wonder. Despite having recently banked the money for Gray, Bhattman couldn't or wouldn't find the £30,000 for Troughton's loan to become permanent and so the young prospect left.

Despite winning at Anfield, we went down without ever looking like doing anything else. Over the next four years the Bhattis sold off every single player who could fetch a price. Consider who Wolves lost: apart from Gray, who went on to inspire Everton to win the Championship, there was Tim Flowers, our England Under-21 'keeper who was 'given' to Southampton for £90,000, and Wayne Clarke, who went to Birmingham for £80,000. Successive managers were forced to use free transfer players, youth opportunities lads, and loan players, as even the less celebrated ones were sold off. All the money for these players, plus that for the social club and training ground, was used to meet winding up orders and debts from any one of several companies in the Bhattis' tangled web of failure.

In 1984 Wolves were in court over non-payment of police bills, and it really seemed like a dying club when Derek Dougan bowed out, disillusioned and embarrassed to have been used by Bhattman as a Trojan horse. Dougan was one of the first to sound the alarm, then Hibbitt and 'Zico' Palmer took Wolves to court over unpaid bonuses accruing from the promotion year two seasons before.

Wolves fans did what fans do in such circumstances – they stopped going. At the start of the 1980s Wolves averaged a 25,000 gate for home league games. Our home average for 1985–6, the season which ended in relegation from the Third Division, was a wee bit over 4000. It wasn't so much watching the team lose, more knowing before practically every game that they would be beaten badly by a club that we fans had hitherto known only from the football pools. It wasn't snobbishness – we just weren't being given time to adjust our expectations of what men wearing gold shirts can do with a football. Some of them wouldn't have made it into my school team, even as over-age players. Having been in Europe a few seasons before, the humiliation was just too much to bear. There was no pride in the club and so the town withdrew its love, hiding it behind black humour.

Several investigative journalists tried all they knew to unearth exactly who was lurking behind the Bhatti name, what on earth they were doing to turn all these people against the club, what their backgrounds were – anything about them – but none penetrated the veil of secrecy. A *Sun* reporter even hired one of the executive boxes in a bid to grab a photo or an interview, but Bhattman's security sent the intrepid reporter packing. That just left the average fan to naively wonder how much 'fitter and leaner' the club was to become before its unseen owners saw the sense of putting some money into their investment.

Relegation to the Third Division came in 1985, and then in the wake of the Bradford disaster, the North Bank and Waterloo Road sides of Molineux were closed down. New manager Tommy Docherty was sacked two weeks before the players were due to report back to training and left complaining that 'it would be easier to find Lord Lucan or Martin Bormann than the owners of Wolves'.

Something had to be done. They were still our football team. And so a group of fans formed the Wolves Action Committee, convinced that the Bhattis, whoever they were, were out to destroy the club.

The Official Supporters' Club launched the campaign to get the Bhattis out as the team fell with the full force of gravity to the bottom of Division Three. Chairman Albert Bates described how the final straw came after a group of fans from the Action Committee had waited around long after the Bristol Rovers game for the Bhattis to emerge, only for the brothers to 'turn on their heels and run like frightened children' at the sight of the delegation.

Protest leaflets, car stickers and T-shirts were produced and a public meeting fixed in Wolverhampton Civic Centre. I travelled down from Manchester for this meeting, which was packed to the rafters. The atmosphere was tense, fearful and yet determined, with some fans' emotions getting the better of them as they reflected on what had become of Wolverhampton's pride and joy. A demonstra-tion was planned for before a match against Walsall. I was one of about 300 on that day and, a little later on, a delegation of Wolves fans held a peaceful picket outside the Bhattis' Mayfair office in London.

It was us – the fans – who had bitten the bullet, and others gathered round with acts of solidarity: Peerless Press pulled out of publishing the programme because the club had told them there could be no more contributions from the Supporters' Club in view of our campaign; the town council allowed the outlawed supporters' club to hold meetings in the offices it rented in the John Ireland stand at the ground; and even the FA got in on the act, by deciding to take no action over a pitch invasion at Molineux in recognition that it was part of the Bhattis Out Campaign and nothing to do with hooliganism. The bail-iffs did their bit too, but their attempt to seize gate receipts in lieu of bad debts was thwarted by the Bhattis.

The boycott of home matches saw only 2205 turn up at Molineux for a league game against Bury. Just as the campaign began to bite in this way, the first intimation came from the Bhattis that they were pre-pared to sell, albeit at the inflated price of £4.5 million. But it took until the end of the season to rip their claws off the cruelly dismem-bered and barely recognizable body of the once mighty Wolves, Lloyds Bank delivering the final blow when they refused the Bhattis thirty days to repay their £750,000 overdraft.

Re-enter the liquidator, but this time as the avenging Angel. Only during this second receivership in 1986 did the full or fairly full facts about the Bhattis begin to emerge and even then the official receiver had to get a High Court order to gain access to the accounts. A club that had cost £2 million in 1982 was left with assets of £50,000 and debts of £750,000. The reason was that the artful Bhattis had mort-gaged Wolves's assets even before day one, in order to finance buying the club. Now that's what I call a user-friendly purchase plan. They went on from that to raise hundreds of thousands of pounds using these same assets as collateral. Second mortgages were taken out, and no accounts had been published throughout their four-year reign of misrule, in complete breach of company law. Even the official receiver declared himself baffled by which Bhatti companies were real, which fictitious, and which ones owned which others. The elder brother Mahmud, it transpired, had received a fifteen-month prison sentence in 1979 for his part in a clothing scandal. Up until the 1980s support-ing a football club did not involve understanding high finance and company law. Many football fans got by without knowing who owned 'their' club. We had no option – it was not until two years into the regime that Mahmud Bhatti's name had appeared in the club pro-gramme as a listed director alongside those of his puppets.

By this stage, in 1986, I didn't give a damn about Wolves being rele-gated to the Fourth Division: we were rid of the Bhattis. It was like watching a loved one miraculously freed of cancer – horribly weak and a shadow of their former self, but still there. By the time we got to our emaciated, shrivelled club there was very little left at all and a stable condition was still a long way off, as an FA Cup defeat at Chorley was to prove. But survival itself was reason enough to be cheerful.

John Bird, then leader of Wolverhampton Council, was instrumen-tal in putting together a package acceptable to all parties. He per-suaded Wolverhampton Council to buy the ground and give Asda adjacent land to build a hypermarket. In exchange the supermarket chain were to pay off the remainder of the debts, and the builders Gallagher were to pay the league registration fees for the new com-pany, Wolves '86.

And so Wolves were back in business, and with the shell of the hypermarket rising up from the urban blight, Wolves' debts will be discharged by the end of 1990.

There was only one song in the town, to the tune of 'Keep the Red Flag Flying', the proud defiance of 'The Wanderers will never die – we'll keep the gold flag flying high', and over the next three years every ground in the lower divisions echoed to it as our ever increasing travelling army breathed new life into the club.

Even so the darkest hour came just before the new dawn: Chorley didn't just knock Wolves out of the FA Cup after two replays; they outclassed them. Some of the press coverage emphasized our plight by way of a footnote to this humiliation, pointing out that the club had barely managed to scrape together the funds for two West Brom reserves that same week: the £20,000 down payment for Andy Thompson and Steve Bull.

These two local lads saw out most of the 1986-7 winter with the rest of the unconvincing bunch and were still there in February, playing in front of just 3000 people against Stockport. With 10 minutes left the game was suddenly transformed by what were to become familiar ingredients in the years to come - a Thommo penalty and a Bully goal. The next week the team won 5-2 at Burnley, and the charge for promotion to the Third Division had begun. Wolves missed out via the play-offs but in the last game of the league programme, Bully became the first Wolves player since John Richards in 1976 to score a hat trick.

The following season, 1987-8, we did go up - as champions, and Stevie Bull got 50 goals. Around the time of his 24th goal, the football press cottoned on to him and fired the first shots in their campaign to sell him to one or other of their favourite clubs. Graham Turner was forced to put up the first of his 'not for sale' signs and Steve himself made the first of his 'Thanks, but no thanks' statements.

One particularly noxious example of this persistent attempt to unsettle Bull and his striking partner Andy Mutch, appeared in the *Daily Mail*, with one of their reporters recounting at great length his conversation with Terry Venables as the pair of them watched Wolves at Reading. It came over like a couple of eighteenth-century slave owners chatting idly at a slave auction about the quality of 'dark meat' on offer. The piece was nothing short of a newspaper providing Venables with a platform from which to declare his interest and name his price - £1.5 million for the pair. Graham Turner, never one to slag off a colleague, said only that he was not sure that this was quite ethical, which was a bit like expressing 'reservations' about concentration camps.

It was the integrity and down-to-earth way in which Steve Bull rejected press speculation that so endeared him to Wolves fans, as well as the wider football public. Bully heaped scorn on the transfer system and on the prices some clubs are willing to pay: 'I'm simply doing the job I'm paid to do, in the same way as a factory worker or a clerk, and they don't have any values placed on them.'

Having worked long shifts in factories himself, Steve was acutely and unusually aware of how privileged the life of a footballer is, at whatever level; he didn't need to be taken down a pit or round a factory to be shown how supporters earn the money which pays his wages. One broken marriage had taught him the value of friendships and family support, and he continually emphasized this aspect when explaining why he didn't want to move away from the Black Country. Journalists, particularly sports journalists preoccupied with the money side of football, found this hard to take in, but thousands of ordinary fans saw in it a refreshing reflection of life as most of us know and live it, and a commonsensical rebuttal of the naive, materialistic dreams which have teased and tormented footballers from Charlie Nicholas to Paul Gascoigne.

Having once received medical advice that his knee would never stand up to professional football and yet going on to play for England, Bully knows all about triumph and disaster and the importance of treating those two imposters just the same – whenever he scores at the North Bank end he wheels round to celebrate in front of and with the fans in the disabled enclosure. When the England Under-21 team played out in Poland, Bully didn't just drag colleague David Burrows down to the bar after the match for a drink with the England fans who had travelled so far to see their country play, he led the singing!

As the late John Lennon put it, a working-class hero is something to be, but it is not a cap to wear if it doesn't fit comfortably and naturally. Along with Bryan Robson, Bully is the only current player with the character as well as the skills of the classical football hero. After the bitter disillusion of the Bhatti years there was no way the Wolves supporters would stomach anything less than cast-iron integrity from anyone wearing gold and black. Bully is a hero with what it takes for the exact time and place into which he has emerged.

In 1988, two years after the avenging angel saved us, 80,000 people from Wolverhampton and Burnley used the occasion of the Sherpa Van Trophy Final at Wembley to celebrate our respective clubs' survival in the league. (Burnley had nearly gone through the trap door to the GM Vauxhall Conference we thought had been purpose built for us.) The Football League and the Wembley authorities seriously underestimated the demand for tickets in Wolverhampton and the Black Country, and had to keep on printing more and more batches as the club kept selling out to the eager punters. With a sadly typical lack of feel for what this match had come to symbolize in the West Mid-lands, the league refused Central Television permission to broadcast it live, even though ticket sales had long since outdistanced their own expectations. Instead, television viewers got pictures of Chelsea fans invading the pitch at a play-off that same weekend. You couldn't have got a more contrasting image of the game and its part in British life.

The 1988 Sherpa Van Final was probably the last great people's occasion at Wembley before it was turned over to the barren spirit of Yuppiedom with Olympic galleries and all-seater ends. None of this desecration had got underway. The last time Wolves had been there, in 1980 for the League Cup Final, seemed to me entirely unconnected with the post-Bhatti Wolves who were about to come through the tunnel into the arena. Although all the pre-match build-up had revolved around the great Wolves and Burnley sides of thirty years before, the Bhatti years stood between all those yesterdays and Graham Turner's Wolves like an unbridgeable fissure, in a curiously parallel way to how Thatcher separates us off from the old industrial Britain. The past counted for nothing in 1986: when Wolves took to the field against the rest of the Fourth Division it was as equals. The club was starting again from scratch; nothing survived the Bhatti years except the dormant pride of the Black Country in the gold and black.

It was that love and pride which gave Wolves the extra edge in the lower divisions, as our supporters filled grounds that hadn't had a capacity league crowd since the National Health Service was created. It was better than playing at home, because home was two ghostly stands from a bygone time, a South Bank with bigger fences than the old Berlin wall, a baseball pitch and a stand too far.

Football is the people's game in this rain-sodden land of ours, and long may it remain so, especially in Wolverhampton. Before any pro-fessional footballer set foot on that Wembley pitch for the Sherpa Van Final against Burnley, the roof was nearly blown off to my right by the legions of Wolverhampton people celebrating our spiritual survival. Whatever Graham Turner's team goes on to achieve, it will never quite match the exhilaration and intensity of feeling in that mighty roar which welled up:

'Hello, Hello . . . Wanderers are back, Wanderers are back.'

Robert Elms

Queen's Park Rangers v *Slovan Bratislava (1977) may not be writ large in the history of English football, but it is the memory of Robert Elms, a QPR supporter all his life, and a mourner for the days of Marsh and Bowles. Around consistent home and away attendance he has fitted in a novel,* In Search of the Crack, *regular appearances on Radio Four's 'Loose Ends', becoming a contributing editor to* The Face, *and written for a number of national newspapers and magazines.*

No More Heroes

ROBERT ELMS

Freedom lies in being bold

Robert Frost

Whenever a television company makes a documentary about a journey to some exotic corner of the world, they always miss out the one I made every week from Burnt Oak, on the outer reaches of the Northern Line, to Loftus Road in deepest Shepherds Bush.

The epic nature of this trek was magnified by the fact that hordes of loud local youths, including my two misguided elder brothers, gathered every alternate Saturday to make the relatively simple trip from our council estate to Highbury, and the glory of the Gunners. Quite why I began to travel in the opposite direction to see a Second Division side called Queen's Park Rangers play at a stadium that still had a mud bank where one stand should be and a crowd that smelled of Old Holborn, is buried in my family history. But the joy that kept me waiting for a number 52 bus throughout a series of sodden, spiteful winters, could be summed up in one profoundly resonant word – Rodney.

His picture hung above my bed of course. In a classic late 1960s pose, his blond hair curled Bryonically over the shoulders of a long-collared, floral shirt, undone at the neck, and his eyes shone impishly. Rodney Marsh was the embodiment of cheeky, carefree athleticism, a number 10 who wore his hooped jersey predictably outside his shorts and his unpredictable ball skills like a banner of buccaneer intent. I, as a pre-teenager in love, could do no more than wonder at the marvel of the man and chant his name with that prolonged, almost melancholic 'O'. We sang 'Roooodney', and Rodney danced.

I first saw his magical footwork in the famed (well it was in my house) 1966–7 season when Rangers won the League Cup and promotion to the Second Division in one season, scoring more than 100 goals on the way. I was taken along to their grubby little football ground in the middle of the even more shabby White City Estate by my dad, who had been a QPR supporter all his life, a life that was to end before the next season started.

Many of his and my mum's relatives lived in the streets around Loftus Road: bus drivers, gas men and Ernie, who had been in the navy. So there were numerous uncles and cousins on hand to see Rodney, wearing an unfamiliar all-white strip, score a magnificent, snaking, Wembley goal. That goal gave my Third Division side a 3–2 victory over First Division big boys West Brom, and meant the League Cup was theirs. That day also gave me a powerful image of a team of contemporary Davids beating the giants with a combination of skill and heart. Deep down, that is still what Rangers mean to me.

As a seven-year-old I was considered too young to go to so big a game. I had to sit with the women in my nan's house, about 400 yards from Loftus Road, and watch on the television. I was therefore robbed of seeing with my own eyes what was probably Rodney's finest hour. In the years that followed I was to see enough to more than make up for it.

By supporting QPR I was perpetuating the tradition of a father who was taken away from the world while still a young man with three young sons. The others were already die-hard Arsenal fans, who had red and white deep in their culture and a Double season just around the corner. They'd been dragged to QPR, but preferred the allure of the local side with its marble halls. I, though, stuck with the Rangers, who were promoted to the First Division in the season following their Cup success. It was then I started to make regularly the tortuous cross-town journey.

Rodney was injured for the first dozen games and we ended up with a record lowest ever 18 points and a ticket back to the real world. I knew then what it was like to taste the bitter joy of supporting a losing team, to run the spiteful Monday morning playground gauntlet. I also knew that it didn't really matter.

It wasn't about winning (though winning is surely sweet). For me and my cousin Ian, another west London exile, living in a prefab in Bethnal Green, Rangers were family. And you don't disown your family just because they're not a huge success. We travelled together and we were part of something. Once that kind of commitment is in your soul, something as superficial and fleeting as success seems less important than being there and living it. When we won though, and Chelsea and Fulham lost, we were kings of the West. It is good to be king for a Saturday.

As the 1960s turned into the 1970s, the only trophy that QPR regularly displayed in the pre-season photo was something called the West London Cup which involved beating Hayes Town and looked like a hub cap stuck on a lump of wood. But it was an honour to stand on that rather unromantic terrace known as the Loft and watch Mr Marsh do his stuff. The drop of the left shoulder, the swerve of the hip that could leave bovine defenders lying in the mud, the nutmeg executed in his own half for the sheer wanton joy of it; a foot placed on the ball, hands on hips with all the ease and the time only the truly inspired can make for themselves. The teasing gesture with both hands to say: come and get it if you really want it. They did, only they never could. Then of course there were the goals: roaring volleys from outside the area, seemingly impossible runs beating half-a-dozen men, some of them twice, before doubling back and rounding a poor goalkeeper; implausible lobs and perfect chips. He did things, you must understand, that players just shouldn't be able to do, and he did them with a smile.

Anybody who has seen the televised hat trick Rodney Marsh scored against Birmingham City in 1970 will know what Marsh was like at the upper reaches of his range. The first goal saw him drop a defender by feinting a through ball, knock the ball up in the air with his left foot, before volleying gloriously home from outside the area with his right. The second was a rare, but perfect header on the run, and the third was a dream. Just inside the box he received the ball, surrounded by defenders; he beat one with a shimmy, another with a dragback, and scored by shooting through the legs of a third. Life can be wonderful.

We didn't win any trophies that year but we played great football, and on those days when it clicked we played a kind of football that made bitter old men from East Acton smile a little. It made me soar.

I am still chafed by the injustice of Rodney Marsh only playing nine times for England. But in the days of Best and Osgood, Law and Baxter, we took skill sadly for granted, and actually applauded the muscular automata of Alf Ramsey's World Cup side as a paragon of modern football. So it is no surprise that after a number of years of delighting the good folk of Shepherds Bush, but being considered too individualistic for the international stage, Rodney hankered for a move to a 'big' club. We had a couple of bad years, and despite many tears shed on the terraces, our Rodney signed for Big Mal's Manchester City. Well you know what it feels like to lose a love? Football, I didn't think, could ever be the same again.

I was in mid-teenage now, and the legs and hips of girls were beginning to distract me from those on the football field. I was still going, but it didn't burn like before. I blame that for robbing me of any memory of Stanley Bowles's first game in the blue and white hooped shirt. I'm sure I was there, but my mind was probably dwelling on Melanie Davison in the third year.

Rangers bought this talented but reputedly wayward young man from sunny Carlisle with little fanfare. Ironically though he had begun his career at Manchester City and their manager Joe Mercer once said that at seventeen he would have played Stanley against the rest of the team and bet on him to win, but he was such trouble that he had to let him go. When he arrived at QPR in 1972 for £110,000 I didn't think much of it. Even the fact that his hair was almost blond, his shirt crept out of his shorts and it carried the number 10, did not make me realize how far Stanley would go in taking Rodney's place.

Marsh and Bowles played in the same spirit but their styles differed. Marsh was more muscular, a big flowing man of obvious intelligence who had the kind of laconic, strolling cheek of those who find life easy. Bowles was a very different character, small, puckish, filled it seemed with demons who could only be exorcised by a good win at the dogs or by taunting defenders with his remarkable skills. Stanley was quick where Rodney was langorous, his footwork was tight and precise where Rodney's was expansive. Marsh painted for a hobby and went on to become a millionaire in America, Stanley gambled and now signs on in Brentford. Both had complete control over a football.

When Stanley Bowles began to turn in a series of incredible solo performances in the mud of Loftus Road, you knew that the spirit of that number 10 shirt, the spirit somehow of the club itself, had been passed on.

Now 1973, we were back in the First Division, and between them consecutive managers Gordon Jago and Dave Sexton had developed a side with a lot more than just one impish wonderkid. It went: Parkes, big sound and safe in goal. The late Dave Clement as an elegant, refined fullback, with the always professional Gillard the other. In the centre of defence, Frank McLintock's wisdom complemented Dave Webb, our cockney conscience. In midfield, there was Gerry Francis, who made his debut at sixteen and was England captain six years later; Don Masson, old Scottish, immobile, and perhaps the most accurate playmaker in British football at the time, and the dependable home boy Mickey Leach. Up front there was Dave Thomas, a quicksilver winger from the Burnley school; a nimble, Irish thoroughbred of a centre forward, by the name of Don Givens. And Stanley Bowles, the finest inside forward I have ever seen. That eleven, six of them in the England side, nine of them internationals, became a holy litany to me in the mid-1970s. (Bowles, like Marsh, was underemployed by England, winning only five caps at a time they couldn't qualify for World Cups.) It was also, for one wonderful season, the most technically advanced and aesthetically pleasing British team of its age.

Statistics don't really tell lies, but liars do tell statistics, and you would have to be a liar, a Liverpudlian or both to deny that Rangers deserved the title in 1975–6. Liverpool won it in the last 14 minutes of the last match at Wolves, robbing Rangers and Stanley Bowles of deserved reward for the style of football they played. 'Total football' was a phrase much in vogue at the time, and there was a decidedly Dutch mobility and arrogance about our play, and especially about Stanley, who revelled in the fact that he now had a perfect platform for his talents.

He did wonderful things: an injury time free kick in the Fifth Round of the Cup bent improbably left footed around a wall to take us through; a magnificent hat trick at Derby, that included two runs from our own half; against Peter Shilton, the coolest piece of forward play I have ever seen: in a one-on-one situation with the best goalkeeper in the world, rooted upright, holding his ground, Stanley dummied him, sending the 'keeper flying to the left while our man casually placed it the other way.

The journey across town wasn't hard that year, nor were the trips to every away game. I would have gone as far as the most committed travelling Glaswegian fan to see the things that our Stanley was attempting. With his grin displaying just a hint of evil, he took defences apart, left them spinning, then did it again, just to wind them up. He knew his time had come, that everything he touched would turn to footballing gold, that this was his season. Deep down you knew what you were watching was unrepeatable.

After a season of magnificence it all came unstuck in our last away game at Norwich. I was just one drop of an ocean of blue and white that travelled to the east that day. Proud we were of our side and of the support for such an unfashionable team. That rural market town became a raging, ringing, carnival outpost of W12 for the day, filled with the old and the young, with all those who had the Rs in their history. This was one of three matches left and if we won them all, we won the league. Perhaps we were overconfident, perhaps of course the Gods decided that QPR didn't win things after all, but we lost 3–2 (to a disgracefully offside goal) and let Liverpool in to win it by one point. I have rarely been so sad and so moved in my life. David didn't make it this time.

The following year we almost made it in Europe. We got knocked out in the quarter-final of the UEFA Cup in faraway Athens, beaten on penalties, and remarkably Stanley Bowles missed one. In the earlier rounds though he'd equalled the eleven-goal record for anybody in that competition and played his part in a spectacular demolition of Slovan Bratislava (which included half the Czech European Nation's Cup-winning side) that was described by one critic as 'the finest performance ever by an English team in Europe'. That game will live with me for ever, as a paragon of sporting excellence, of fluid, faultless football. Rangers destroyed one of the continent's finest teams 5–2, after drawing away 3–3.

The team was still a good one but missed the consistency of the year before. One year later it had gone. And before long Stanley had gone too. He slowed down a little, became, I would guess, disenchanted with playing in a struggling team, and ended up moving to Nottingham Forest. If ever a player was pathologically unsuited to Mr Clough's authoritarian style of management it was Stanley Bowles. I also believe he missed London and especially the White City, where he had probably always felt most at home. Anyway, it didn't work out with Forest and after a while he ended up via Orient at Brentford, playing in midfield, and by all accounts playing with ten times more grace and style, elegance and excellence than anyone had seen in thirty years at Griffin Park.

He still had something. In Spanish there's a word for this, called *duende*. Literally translated it means 'he is with the elves and imps' – he has a certain magic. In English there is no real equivalent, but in football you know it when you see it. *Duende* is that indefinable, intangible quality that goes beyond skill, beyond even brilliance, it is the stuff that heroes are made of. And in Rodney Marsh and Stanley Bowles QPR were graced with two number 10s who had enough *duende* for a whole side. Without them my team just doesn't seem the same. A preening, vainglorious footballer known as Simon Stainrod acted as pretender to that mantle for a while. Another, John Byrne, a likeable but never-quite-there Irishman, also had a go, but neither of them really had the skill nor the charisma.

Rangers are still my team of course, and in Paul Parker they have a player who consistently comes close to perfection as a defender. I still go to most home and many away matches, still care to the core of my soul. But it feels at times when you watch mortal footballers doing their imperfect stuff, that the number 10 shirt should have been retired long ago, as in baseball when a great player finishes his career.

I have also tried watching football away from Loftus Road. During an extended sojourn in Barcelona, I headed regularly for Nou Camp, and the team that carries the pride of Catalonia on its back. There were some great and gifted footballers on display, (and if they were playing Réal, passion of a kind we will never know). At times too there were technical skills way beyond anything we see in the hurried, physical melee of our league game. But for me, despite my intense love of that city, and despite doing my best to drum up some desire, my heart wasn't in it, and after a while I found myself forsaking the Sunday routine of a trip to the football for an afternoon at the bullring.

Back in England, I no longer live in Burnt Oak. In fact I have moved even closer to Highbury, and most of my mates and both my brothers are still Arsenal supporters. I will admit that there have been times in the last few, fairly barren years, when I've gone to bed at night praying to wake up supporting the Gunners, to feel another colour in my heart. I know it will never happen of course, it simply isn't possible; you can change anything in life except the football team you support. It would make life a lot easier though, and it would be nice to see my team actually win something for once.

It would be nicer still to have someone back at QPR who could stand with a football at his feet and make you tingle with anticipation. When I can't sleep at night, because of workaday worries running round my adult mind, I transport myself back to some sunny day at Loftus Road when I was a teenager and Rodney, or Stanley, those two footballing geniuses, were tormenting the opposition with their talents. In a blur of blue and white they turn circles of elegance, deliver passes of excellence and score goals of spellbinding elan. Everything at that moment is right and proper and this humble muddy game of ours has elevated us all.

By way of an epilogue, I have just watched a £1 million-man playing for Queen's Park Rangers. The blue and white hooped shirt now bears an ugly corporate motif on the front, and this man had black hair instead of blond, but there were a few portentous moments. He tried things that seemed almost quaint in our modern game, like beating a man. He juggled even, and swerved, and I thought I spotted a grin on his face just once. The number 10 on his back didn't seem entirely out of place. It's too early to say of course, and I may be dreaming again. But could it be Rodney, Stanley and Wegerle.

Geoff Dyer

People from Cheltenham have trouble deciding which team to support, and it was really by chance that Geoff lent his affections to Chelsea. And it was by chance that only when rejected by every major advertising agency in London did Geoff have the time to write. In 1989 his first novel, The Colour of Memory, *was published, and he is currently living in New York working on a book about jazz,* Alternate Takes, *to be published in 1991.*

Chelsea, Cheltenham

GEOFF DYER

[John] Moynihan strolled around the table, expertly flipping the little toy football-figures, scoring goal after goal, while David, large in shirt-sleeves and braces, bustled round the table crying, 'Oh, f - - -, f - - -!'

Brian Glanville, foreword to *The Soccer Syndrome*

There is a genre of conversation people tend to fall into at moderately unsuccessful dinner parties; the idea is to delight each other with – and spur each other on to – ever more detailed and affectionate memories of ice creams (Skyray, Heart, Zoom), or television programmes: 'Ripcord', 'The Rat Patrol' (someone always points out it was banned after complaints from veterans of the Eighth Army). Successful recollection conveys automatic affection on the object/ craze/programme in question: 'D'you remember loons?'

'Oh they were great, I had a pair with . . .' The more precise the memory the more intense the affection it generates. (Remembering the series 'Robinson Crusoe' someone always says 'I loved the music' and hums the theme tune or points out that it went out after 'Jackanory' and before 'Blue Peter'.) Ideally the memory should be so contingent on individual circumstance as to leave listeners astonished that they too are touched by it, that they too are included within its orbit.

There is a similar temptation when thinking about a favourite foot-ball team – in my case the Chelsea side of the early 1970s – to list the names of the players, describe their haircuts and particular quirks of play, recall key sequences of results or moments on the path to Cup or League glory or failure.

Aside from the fact that man for man they had what is probably the most impressive collection of sideburns of any team since the Victor-ian era, I am surprised by the vagueness of my memory of early 1970s' Chelsea.

101

The team:

Peter Bonetti: the cat, got hurt by Mick Jones in the FA Cup Final against Leeds, deputized for Gordon Banks against West Germany in the Mexico World Cup and let in the soft goals that resulted in England getting knocked out.

Eddie McCreadie: my aunt's lover gave me a used Cup Final ticket with his signature on it.

John Dempsey: I remember absolutely nothing about him apart from the fact that he played for Eire. A solid defender, I assume.

David Webb: a defender who loved to come forward, as they say. Scored the winning goal in the Cup Final replay against Leeds in 1970, yeti-style hair and beard. Prominent dimple on chin.

Ron Harris: chopper, captain, hard man, scored a goal once.

Charlie Cooke: the wizard of the dribble, Scottish. Already at the peak of his career by the time I became interested in football.

Peter Houseman: winger, short hair, scored a goal against Leeds because Sprake fumbled – it still makes me laugh. Unpopular with the fans for some reason.

Peter Osgood: the star player, probably the longest and thickest sideburns on the team, crinkly hair, loped around the centre circle doing nothing for large parts of the game and then did something skil-ful. Broke his leg once, played for England a couple of times in minor matches (one of them abandoned because of bad weather). Worked as a labourer before turning professional and, like many footballers, hankered after country squire existence.

Ian Hutchinson: sideburns of near-Osgood proportions. A huge throw with windmill arms.

Alan Hudson: glamorous, long hair, the darling of the King's Road. Along with Arsenal's Charlie George (much longer hair) was Lon-don's (slightly belated) answer to George Best. Perfect example of how early 1970s' fashion – big ties with big knots, big collars – achieved its fullest expression in the wardrobes not of pop stars but of First Division footballers. Hudson once scored a goal that was sub-sequently shown to have gone wide of the post but which ricocheted off the netting support and was adjudged by the referee to have gone in.

I know there is one more to make up the team. Who on earth is it? (I am writing this in America – would it be easier to remember in

England?) Oh yes, it's John Hollins; I nearly forgot him. And even now I can't remember anything about him. Number 4?

What else? Nicknamed the Pensioners. Change strip: yellow shirts and socks, blue shorts. The Shed. Came from behind twice against Leeds in the FA Cup Final, final score 2–2 after extra time; won the replay at Old Trafford. Osgood scored a goal. The following year they won the European Cup Winners' Cup against Réal Madrid. Osgood scored again. And that's it.

I grew up not in Chelsea, London, but Cheltenham, Gloucestershire – the midwest as it were. So why Chelsea? Why not a local team? There *was* no local team to speak of. Cheltenham – the Robins, as they were fondly known – were in the Southern League Premier Division and weren't glamorous enough to merit much excitement (my economics teacher at grammar school played for them). More importantly, there was no rule stipulating that you had to live within a team's geographical catchment area in order to support them, so most of us looked further afield. (Midlands Television mistakenly assumed that because Gloucestershire fell in their region we wanted constant exposure to the likes of Coventry, Stoke, Derby, Birmingham, Wolves and Villa; but while TV executives supposed a derby between two of these muddy teams to be the high point of the viewer's season, my friends and I were only interested in watching when they played a team from London or Merseyside.) What was the point in following a Third Division team like Swindon – the nearest league team to Cheltenham – when you could choose a team who picked up a couple of trophies a year? Taking this argument to its logical conclusion a number of kids at school simply supported whichever team won the league or Cup, shifting their allegiances every season. The only restriction was that it was considered preferable to be the first person to support a given team rather than being the sixth or seventh person in class to latch on to Manchester United (Man U) who everyone really wanted to support. In practice this meant that teams were allotted to our affections on a first-come first-served basis, the hierarchy of desirability tying in almost exactly with the frequency with which teams appeared on 'Match of the Day'. If someone switched their support to another side (as frequently happened, often on the basis of a poor performance on 'Sportsnight with Coleman') then there was a rush to jump in and claim the vacant spot and enlist as a follower of the abandoned team. Often a kind of domino effect resulted: someone went from being an Arsenal supporter to a Spurs fan, someone else swapped from Everton to Spurs, and in turn a third person went from Man City to Spurs and so on.

I started off supporting Leeds, a successful team, but it was difficult to muster up much enthusiasm for the likes of Billy Bremner or Jack Charlton. Peter Lorimer was the big attraction – fastest shot in the league – but I always felt drawn towards the London teams. Then one morning Kevin Gibbard came in with the news that a relative of his had been taken on as a goalkeeper for Derby County, thereby causing Kevin to spurn Chelsea and become a fervent fan of the Rams. Like someone hearing of an apartment becoming vacant in a crowded city I jumped in quick, poured scorn on Don Revie's methodical efficiency and declared Chelsea to be my team.

When I say Chelsea were my favourite team I don't mean I supported them so much as collected the merchandising and souvenirs associated with them. My bedroom resembled nothing so much as a colony of Stamford Bridge, the Cheltenham branch of the Supporters Club shop. Pennants, ties, rosettes, lapel badges, bobble hats, scarves, records –

> *Blue is the colour*
> *Football is the game*
> *We're all together*
> *And winning is our aim . . .*

– programmes, posters, mugs, mascots, books (the team annuals, Osgood's autobiography, *Ossie the Wizard*), home-made scrapbooks of press clippings. Ah, collecting – few activities on earth are more fulfilling. My hunger for accumulation did not stop at Chelsea: I collected anything to do with football. Every week I bought *Shoot* and *Goal* (I had a complete run, including even the dummy issue – a cousin who worked in a newsagent in Shrewsbury got it for me) and every month I picked up *Charles Buchan's Football Monthly* (as it was somewhat archaically titled).

Some time towards the end of the 1960s Soccer Stars pictures appeared. For a couple of pence you got a packet with five or six random glossy photos and a pink strip of bubble gum (in exactly the same style as 'James Bond' or 'Man from Uncle' cards). The complete set –

there was an album to stick them in – comprised the first-team squads of every team in the First Division. Some players turned up in practically every packet, others – predictably enough George Best and Bobby Charlton – were especially rare. We stood in the playground, riffling through each others' swap piles with bored familiarity until coming across a face we hadn't seen before: 'Got, got, got, got, got, got, got, got, got, got, NEED!' Then the hard business of transfer negotiation would begin. For a George Best you could get practically the whole of the Fulham team.

Then there was my collection of football games. My mother thought she could make a Subbuteo pitch for a quarter of the price they charged in the shops (she made clothes for my Action Man on the same principle: mine was the only Action Man with a corduroy jacket and beige slacks). All we needed to buy, she said, were two teams, goals and a ball. In the end I got my own way (I always got my own way) and we bought the proper pitch as well. Floodlights, referees and grandstands seemed superfluous but I bought numerous teams, stuck numbers on to the backs of players' shirts and constructed elaborate leagues which imposed a gruelling schedule of play on myself and friends. I was an only child and often had to play on my own, attacking and defending simultaneously. Like most people I played table football on the floor and became angry when friends trod on a player. I was an excellent Subbuteo player and repaired my players carefully with glue from Airfix models. Even now, twenty years later, the pitch is in fine condition, if a little scuffed in the penalty boxes.

At an art gallery recently I saw an installation entitled 'Some People Think It's All Over' which comprised the England and West Germany Subbuteo teams arranged in the positions of the team a few seconds before Geoff Hurst scored England's fourth goal in the 1966 World Cup Final and commentator Kenneth Wolstenholme added 'It is now' to the famous line that gave the piece its title. (Possible essay: 'Subbuteo: sporting history and the table-top simulacrum'.)

Other games. Soccerama: a Monopoly-style board game; soccer from the manager's point of view, endorsed by Alan Ball who I think called it the best game he had ever played (we used to mimic his high-pitched voice).

Penalty: a card game, very old fashioned; minimal packaging, simple rules. The players depicted on the cards wore Stanley Matthews shorts and the goalies (the word has an Alf Tupper ring to it) wore cloth caps.

Wembley: all I can remember is the box and I can't even remember that properly (a goalie in a yellow polo neck diving for the ball?).

In many ways the matches at Stamford Bridge were a pale imitation of Subbuteo (all the thrills and spills of real Subbuteo in the public glare of the park).

In junior school I was picked for a trial for the team. In those days of 5–3–2 the team positions were arranged in descending order of ability: best players forwards, average players in midfield, the worst in defence and somebody absolutely hopeless in goal: I wore the number 2 shirt even though I never liked tackling. Chelsea shorts had white stripes down the sides so my mother sewed them on for me, one on each side. My father bought me a leather ball with laces. A relic of bygone days even then, it felt like a bag of sugar when you headed it and the laces cut into your forehead.

George Best football boots came on the market: purple, side-lacing, twice as expensive as any other pair. 'You're paying for the name,' said my mother, shaking her head in Terry Warner's Sports. I didn't even want a pair but I still wanted a pair. We compromised with a pair of Puma screw-ins. It was essential to have screw-ins though nobody was sure why. Better for turning was one explanation. Also they had white soles and looked elegant as you ran. As soon as I got home I took them out of the box and tissue paper and walked around the bedroom in them as though they were carpet slippers. I unscrewed the studs with the little metal spanner. After I screwed them back in I never took them out again and never bought another pair of studs but persisted in playing – whether the ground was slate-hard with frost or soft as battlefield mud – with the original six nylon studs. Boots with very low ankles and long floppy tongues were becoming popular.

At grammar school the official game was rugby but once a term they would allow us to play soccer on the rutted Somme of a rugby pitch: terrible games, twenty-a-side, with the goals so colossal the 'keeper stood no chance of making a save. The rest of the time we played in the playground, as many as twenty games going on in an area about half the size of a normal pitch. A crossfire of balls smacking you in the face on a cold day, players in other games charging you down. . . . The dawn of the global hegemony of the training shoe. Two captains would line up and pick teams. The best players kicked the ball around without taking any notice, confident of being chosen quickly, the worst looked abject. To avoid the embarrassment of being picked last the very worst often became captains themselves. On Saturday after-noons we trudged around town, watching the football results through the window of the TV rental shop.

Mexico 1970: the high altitude technicolour of yellow shirts and blue shorts, the green haze of the pitch, the satellite crackle of David Coleman's voice coming from across the other side of the world. The time difference meant that some games were shown in the morning before school. Pelé chesting the ball down and volleying it home, shooting from the halfway line (and missing), dummying the goalkeeper and scoring. . . . (Or did he score? Concentrating very hard I can see the ball sliding past the post. The *unforced* memory is certainly of a goal. In other words the manoeuvre was so audacious that it has dummied memory, perfecting itself in recollection.) Brazil: Pelé, Jairzinho, Tostao. When I think of soccer that is what I think of. When I think of England in Mexico I think of Bobby Moore getting arrested in Bogota, Alf Ramsey . . . Alf Ramsey doing what? Well, nothing, just being Alf Ramsey, wearing a shiny tracksuit and looking like a shy man who lives with his widowed mother well into middle age.

I was a reasonable player who could never rise to the occasion. When-ever there was a big match in the Sunday league (unruly, frequently violent affairs) I would miss a sitting chance at goal and look over at my father, a stoical figure in cloth cap and blue anorak, apparently unconcerned that his considerable paternal pride had no more tal-ented object than myself on which to focus. If I didn't get the ball for five or ten minutes I sulked, wandering round the pitch aimlessly and looking down at the patterns of stud marks in the grim drizzle of the recreation park. (Is the technology available to recreate forensically the exact sequence of play in a game from the stud patterns in the pitch? A sort of archaeological action replay?)

I can't remember exactly when I started losing interest in foot-ball. The usual explanation for abandoned athletic aspirations is discovering girls. For me it was books. Games afternoons I'd slope off and do my English homework instead. Also, as sometimes happens, the sudden spurt of testosterone that surges through adolescents had an odd – though frequently observed – side effect on me: I rocketed up to 6 ft and put on no weight. My legs were like daffodil stalks and I tried to avoid any activities which involved taking off my trousers (I played squash in jeans).

If I had never liked tackling then I hated heading the ball, especially from goalkeepers' clearances. Typically, I jumped into the air but sunk my neck into my shoulders in order to miss the ball. By the time of my last games when I was sixteen, 6 ft 2 in-tall defenders would point to me at corners, shouting 'Watch the big man' as I prowled round the 6-yard box looking aerially menacing and hoping I had managed to position myself at a safe distance from the probable trajectory of the ball.

Ten years later I rediscovered football. Predictably enough it started with a quiet game of Subbuteo with a few close friends – everyone very impressed by how well preserved my pitch was – and from there we progressed to a kick-around, after which, lying in the park smoking grass, Paul said, 'The invention of the ball was one of the milestones of human evolution, probably more important than the invention of the wheel.' John, a keen cyclist, disagreed but I liked the sense of something epochal and fundamental this observation imparted to subsequent games. Not only that but since many of my contemporaries were starting to look like they'd swallowed a pastry grenade I was actually quite pleased with my Bambi-esque legs. Also, over the previous four years I'd built up a bad squash habit and had arrived at the conclusion that I'd missed my vocation in life: I wasn't meant to be a low-income intellectual, I was a natural sportsman – my early prowess at Subbuteo was proof of that – and I jumped at every opportunity to show my co-ordination, speed and fitness. Sport, physical competition, that was the key to human happiness.

I played football more and more frequently until, after months of speculation, we succeeded in organizing regular eleven-a-side games on Clapham Common every Sunday. This was such a success that ten of us made a firm commitment and booked a five-a-side pitch at the Ferndale Centre in Brixton. Only five of us turned up so we played some guys who were hanging around looking for a game. The two sides were very easy to distinguish from each other: they were all black, we were all white; they displayed considerable skill and team-work, we showed none; they wore state-of-the-art trainers, we made do with old tennis shoes and plimsolls. They mounted elaborately planned attacks that tended to break down on the edge of the penalty area. The lack of teamwork on our own side was such that the word team was utterly inappropriate to the anarchic every-man-for-himself ethic that prevailed. Typically one of our team would get the ball and try to dribble as far as possible before taking a wild pot in the general direction of the goal while the rest of the team yelled, 'Pass it, bloody pass it.' Both teams played with a rotating goalkeeper – one person staying in goal until he let one in. Whoever was in goal at their end made spectacular saves while anyone in goal on our side did every-thing possible to avoid blocking even the feeblest shot so that he could get out on the pitch again.

This contrast in approach lasted for perhaps half an hour and then, seeing that their tactics were no more successful than our lack of them – for every ten shots we thundered over the bar one would go in – they resorted to long-range shooting and speculative blasts. By a gradual consensus we abandoned the rule about no shooting from inside your own half. Then we overturned the rule which stipulated that the ball must not go above head height – superfluous since the only time the ball came *below* head height was when someone was about to boot it back into the air again. In the end their team lined up in front of their goal and we lined up in front of ours, taking it in turns to bombard each other with long shots. At some point a second ball came into play, fol-lowed by a third and fourth and soon we were firing upwards of half a dozen balls back and forth like German and English troops tossing mortars at each other across the no-man's-land of the pitch. Gradually all the balls but one were booted clear of the perimeter fence and when the last one bounced out into the road this not uninteresting variant of soccer came to an end, leaving both teams to ponder the alle-gorical significance of what had taken place.

This revival of interest in soccer coincided with an era of rabid anti-patriotism: wanting England to lose because they played the most boring football in the world but knowing they were going to scrape by on some mathematical miracle. In this respect our finest hour was not the 1966 World Cup Final but the draw with Morocco in Mexico in 1986 when Butch Wilkins got sent off for petulance.

For the big internationals we'd gather round the TV, John, Paul, Charlie and me, get high and sip slim bottles of beer imported from whichever country England happened to be playing. Transmitted live from a country with an atrocious human rights record, the game would ideally be the first leg of the preliminary round of the qualifying sec-tion of the World Cup eliminators – an important game for England since if they drew it would mean that in the forthcoming game against Sweden they would have to make sure that they didn't lose by a margin of more than five goals unless Scotland beat Albania by at least two goals in which case they had only to keep the defeat down to a single figure difference in order to qualify:

'God, I hope we don't win.'

'I hope we get really hammered.'

'Thrashed, trounced, slaughtered, annihilated, pissed on.'

'I hope Lineker never even sees the ball.'

'I hope Robson does a gentle pass back and Shilton lets it slip through his fingers.'

'Then I hope there's a riot and the English fans are banned from not just Europe but from all competition for ever, world without end.'

One such game got under way with a foul in the first minute. The England trainer sprinted on to the pitch and the game was held up for two minutes while he attended to the injured player.

'So far we've had 10 seconds of play and 2 minutes of injury time. I wonder if that's a record,' complained John.

'You misunderstand the nature of the modern game,' said Paul. 'The magic sponge provides no relief, it's superfluous. Similarly scoring goals is only of secondary importance. What really counts is how fast the trainer can run to the injured player. That is where the true con-test of the modern game lies. We've got off to a magnificent start, Brian.'

When the free kick was taken the ball was headed straight into touch and bobbled towards the spectators who looked like political prisoners behind the wire perimeter fence and moat. From then on most of the action was confined either to the running track surround-ing the pitch as tracksuited youths reluctantly retrieved the ball, or to the centre circle where players congregated for goal kicks and then elbowed, nudged, pushed or tripped each other until a free kick was awarded or the ball bounced harmlessly off the pitch into long rows of empty seats. The stadium was two-thirds empty; close-ups of corner kicks often failed to reveal a single spectator within the wide-angle of the camera.

It soon became apparent that the bright afternoon sunshine of Eastern Europe had divided the pitch lengthways into two halves, one of psychedelic brightness, the other of Golgothian shadow so dark that nothing could be seen until the cameras were apertured up and the bright half of the pitch bleached ice-hockey white. Occasionally there was a round of applause, activated, it seemed, by dismal blasts on a lone claxon. Here and there in the non-crowd were a few soldiers who looked surly and bored as if resenting taking time off from torturing dissidents.

A few minutes into the second half Lineker was brought down a few yards beyond the edge of the box. The English team protested that it should have been a penalty but, much to the disgust of the commentator, the referee was adamant that only a free kick was merited. The opposition skulked around and set up a defensive wall a little more than 18 inches from the spot where the kick was due to be taken. Dragging the wall back the full 10 yards took just over 8 minutes, during which time, more in frustration than anger, an English player whacked the ball straight into their collective – and as yet unprotected – testicles and was promptly booked. When the kick was eventually taken the ball ricocheted off the crossbar, disturbing a bird who, to the delight of cameramen and commentators alike, had been perched there for most of the match and showed every sign of having been soundly asleep.

England's goal, when it eventually came in the 70th or so minute, was something of a farce. Intercepting a low cross with a reckless excess of enthusiasm the opposition number 3 thumped the ball past his own goalkeeper with a left foot volley so exquisitely placed that it could have passed for an act of treason. For the last 20 minutes of the game the opposition threw themselves into niggling tackles while England passed the ball back and forth in their own half and embarked on a series of substitutions so comprehensive that by the time of the final whistle it seemed that Shilton was the only member of the original team to remain on the field.

The next day I tore the ligaments in my ankle. Disaster: no squash, running or football for ten weeks. In fact no football ever again. As I recovered and watched games on television the real purpose and meaning of football became clear to me: to tear the ligaments in your ankle. Everything about the game – tackling, blocking, dribbling – leads inexorably to torn ankle ligaments.

As for Chelsea, I could only name a couple of players in the team, though I do know the name of the chairman: Ken Bates. They are one of those teams who get promoted one year and relegated the next so that their real home is the limbo between divisions. Oh yes, and a couple of years ago I thought I saw Ian Hutchinson on a train. I thought about mentioning that earlier but since I can't be sure and didn't speak to him at the time – he was drinking a can of Heineken – I decided against it. There's all sorts of other stuff I didn't mention as well: the fact that my cousin was married to Kevin Reeves who played for Norwich and Manchester City, that Mike Summerbee went to the same junior school as me. . . . No, if you want all that stuff you have to see it live and that, as anyone who has watched 'The Match' on a Sunday afternoon will tell you, is often a bit of a bore. I have always preferred the highlights. These were my highlights, the bits I remember, the best bits.

Richard Jobson

A Scottish schoolboy star and player for Aston Villa Boys Club in his home town of Glasgow, Richard might have been a footballer if pop stardom hadn't got in the way at the tender age of sixteen, when his band 'The Skids' hit the big time. A follower of Celtic, he describes Parkhead as his family's church. Since hanging up his microphone, Richard has published a book of poetry and a book about Glasgow. He presents '01-For London' on television and is a regular contributor to Radio Four's 'Loose Ends'.

The Trial

RICHARD JOBSON

Macbeth: Who can be wise, amazed, temperate and furious
Loyal and neutral, in a moment? No man . . .

Macbeth, Act II, Scene 3

The ball drifted slowly into the zone I was defending. To my right, on the touchline, stood my father, brother and uncle. To my left stood the school's team coach, his assistant and a man dressed in a sheepskin coat and sunglasses. He had to be an Arsenal scout. The big English clubs often sent their talent spotters up north to assess schoolboys. Get them young was the idea. Take them south, mess them up and send them packing up north again. Being looked at by an English club was every boy's dream. Heading south. The thought encouraged the imagination to go wild. Cries were heard from the North Bank, 'We love you Jobbo, we do!' Screams from the Shed, 'The Chin is gonna get you!' And chants from the Stretford End, 'There's only one Richie Jobson!'

I could hear this noise, I could feel the eyes of the mystery scout and most importantly I could sense the angst coming from my relations as my left foot came into contact with the ball. The coach had explained that the school would adopt the continental method of football – not roughneck British stuff but a graceful ball-on-the-floor passing game.

The ball came to me. I tapped it ahead slightly, and looked up at the marauding Protestant boys running toward me as if breaching the gates of some Papal palace. F - - - this, I thought, and kicked the ball out of play. I had panicked; terrified of the oncoming Prods. I lamely looked at the touchline. The eyes behind the sunglasses were talking to me: 'Would Franz Beckenbauer have done that?' No. But Jim Holton would have. And besides Beckenbauer had a rotten haircut; but so did Jim Holton. I put my fingers through my hair. Perfect. The gel and hairspray had kept the quiff in place and the bum fluff around my cheeks was beginning to look like serious sidies. Any player with a future had to have sidies. In fact, looking the part was half the battle. Who would dare tackle a guy with his falsers in his top pocket, sidies, Nobby Stiles hairdo, no shin pads and with Puma Pelés on? Who?

This guy had style. Like a walking monument, casting shadows on the unworthy. My outfit heralded the coming tackle, the header and now and again the odd goal. It was important to get a bit of mud on your legs and bum early on in the game, sometimes even before the match had started. In fact the pre-match build up could be more important than the game itself. The concentration required to get a semi-stiffy, and not a complete hard-on, was one of life's most severe trials. The reasons behind this were of course to do with footballing vanity. A small cock is definitely the possession of a bad player. All good players have big ones. Me? Well, I was sort of average. But this mediocrity could be dealt with in a single fantastical moment conjured by the thought of my big brother's girlfriend's bra (which I had nicked when they were at it); it could drive this boy into the realm of ecstasy. But at the moment of releasing her heaving hefties my Dad would walk into the room and down, down, down, Charles Aznavour would go. So at this point, when the fantasy had stopped, your boy's wee man was not up but neither was he down. He had reached the kind of proportions which got the respect that I needed from the other players. 'Whoa, he must be a good player,' they thought to themselves, sneaking a look.

The shirt, shorts, stockings and shin pads all played second fiddle to the body ointment, oil of wintergreen. It burnt into the legs a deep heat which made them turn a sudden, glowing pink. So hysterical was this change of colour it gave the anointed the look of a tense, raging bull who would stop at nothing to flatten whatever came in his way. This sudden macho-madness, of course, stemmed from great pain. We ignored that wintergreen was meant to be applied in a smear, not handfuls of the gunk, rubbed hard into calves, thighs and of course, for real men, testicles. The smell was obscene. It could have melted a polar icecap. It could have solved the problems in the Lebanon. It is an unused psychological and physical weapon of great proportions. After the ointment, the kit was put on with a great urgency. The boy was a man in armour, and he was ready for battle. Next location: the pitch.

On this particular day I was playing for my school, St Columbia, the area's only Catholic school, which for some reason held a great tradition of football teams. This could be explained sociologically (Catholics were the poorer members of society), but I put it down to the temperament of our ancestors. All us Catholics in Scotland come from an Irish background. This has lots and lots of minuses: bad drink problems, laziness, red hair, bad tempers. . . . But racism aside, we are also naturally poetic. I obviously don't mean in the written word, I mean in our attitude. As a kid I never had a boring moment. Every day was another story, adventure or mass murder. My parents and five boys in a two-roomed house always seemed to have space. We were out there playing football, talking football, watching football, living football.

Football held a great symbol of what a young Catholic could achieve in this country. Its name was Celtic. Born from the benevolence of the Irish Christian brothers in 1888, in the East End of Glasgow, and using the motif of an Irish shamrock, Celtic were an identity for a lost generation of Irish migrant workers. The feeling that great events could happen in that poor underdeveloped area, with a team who played heart before money and fun before religion has never stopped. The insurmountable dilemmas which have dogged the club's history have only strengthened the world's most loyal and critical support. When the team are doing well, they walk on water and when they are struggling suddenly everybody's an expert and the manager should be replaced with the man from the Bovril stall.

I first witnessed the hoops on their home territory of Celtic Park, or Paradise, when I was five years old. I remember nothing. But for a boy who faced the banality and claustrophobia of a housing estate, the epic, near cinematic glory the club reached in their endeavours to please me and my mates made a Saturday afternoon the equivalent of a trip to Mecca or a snog with Ursula Andress. I grew up in their most glorious period: the first British club to win the European Cup and nine successive league titles. When they attacked it was like Saracen horsemen humiliating clumsy Crusaders. When we played Rangers we were the Infidel and they the Puritan. We were believers, they were just greedy.

I heard things on the football chatline. Half-time talk of girls, and fighting, drinking and life without work caught my ear in the jungle section of Celtic Park. An orgasm wasn't an Israeli orange after all, and the Labour Party were trying to make things better, said the Big Man to the Wee Man; my ears took it all in. Watching Celtic made me want to play football, but never for them; for I knew I just would never be good enough.

From as far back as I remember I have kicked a ball. Even when it was with just a collection of old rags tied together, it became a big match. It took the importance of the international stage. The cameras were there, there was the build-up, the team talk, and the tactics, which were always, Attack! Attack! Attack!

There were lots of goals. Nobody considered being the defender of the realm. Oh no. It was up and on toward glory. A glory which would bring the television cameras and the legendary Archie Macpherson (rumoured to be a hun, but actually a very influential media man).

'Well Dick, what do you remember about the goal?'

'Well Archie, Sean slipped it through to Des, who saw Paddy free on the right, who thumped it across to me in the middle. Unfortunately our goalie was off his line and I nodded it past him.'

Learning how to deal with the media was tremendously important to fourteen-year-old boys. Already terms such as 'the lads', 'the boss' and 'one game at a time', had infiltrated our conversation. Potential hooliganism, which was inherent in all at my school, was not to be touched. Scandals could rock a career at an early stage. One report in the local paper would mean the end of those cold Saturday morning rituals which brought such joy to the neighbourhood. A representative of his school, and future international player, could not be a thieving, spray-painting, glass-breaking, street-fighting man like the rest of his family and friends. He had to be bigger than that.

It was an escape. A way out of misery. Though these serious notes were never thought of at the time. The game just helped give a sense of responsibility to potential criminals. It also opened the door to an organized camaraderie.

'Ya f - - - - -' eedjit,' boomed Murdo, the team captain. This was ironic seeing as he played on one foot that was not connected to his brain. Murdo was fourteen years old, 6 ft and could drink more Scotsmac and Irnbru than any consenting adult I had ever witnessed. This item of aplomb was one he was very proud of. Someone had once written on a steamed up window in the changing room: 'Murdo is

Murder'. That questioned his integrity and ability. He didn't like that. But he didn't trouble himself by asking who had written this slanderous note. No, that wasn't his style. His course of action was much bigger: after a late night practice session he beat up the whole team.

The man was, at heart, a gentle soul, who liked the company of pigeons, ferrets, and fishing rods. He was an earth man, a troglodyte, a basic Neanderthal who couldn't accept that two times two equalled four – it was unfair because it gave him no advantage. Simple but sometimes effective, especially during Cup games, like all men he only really became violent when his manhood came into question. And nobody in their right mind would question the big man. He came from a family of fourteen. The mother was dead. The father was a drunk.

His remark to me had not gone unnoticed by my family. My brother, also big and always angry, replied, 'That's great, coming from you, *le grand merde*'. Even the referee stopped for a moment. Was that Gaelic, Norse or French? This comment had thrown the players into confusion.

I noted the high-collared scout writing something into his wee black book. Could you imagine what the pages of that book had witnessed – Charlie George, George Graham, Super Mac and now, Big Jobbo. At this moment he was probably recording his impressions of the cultural fluidity of the Jobson family. Yes, the man was no fool. He must have understood why I had thumped the ball off the park. What dignity. Putting the ball out of play when I could have carried it up the field on a counter attack.

From my cock-eye, which I had learned to use to my advantage, I saw our coach trying to get the referee's attention with the aim of making a substitution. The boss had decided to bring on a fresh pair of legs to help the lads up front. Our right back was having a nightmare, poor kid, he could probably do with a break. To be substituted was the ultimate humiliation for a player at this level. I had even heard of a player being substituted when there wasn't a player to replace him. Ten men, it would seem, could do a better job than eleven. That slow walk off the park to your team's changing room and the shock of being removed is followed by instantaneous hate for the coach, the team, and football itself. Why me? is always the question banging away like toothache. A substitution could be the final spark in a bad year at school. Suicide beckoned as even bad exam results were over-shadowed. It was an event. A major one. The legs suddenly didn't work as you trudged, head down, to that faraway place, the dressing room. The broken soul dragging his legs like the saddest of men, Captain Ahab. Oh, what misery can be caused by a rash decision.

The boss caught the attention of the referee, who turned to me and said, 'It's you, go on, hurry up. Piss off!'

The man had made a mistake. No, surely not me. It couldn't be. Not today. Why me? It all came upon me like a freak thunderstorm. Every-thing went black, interrupted only by an occasional flash and rumble. Noise and light came from primal motions deep down in my throat. I became a rabid dog. My eyes tried to suppress the tears now falling in disgrace. I hated football, therefore I hated life. This cataclysmic error had uprooted my world and deadened the planet.

Humiliation was then overtaken by inspired thoughts of how to end it all. A nearby cliff, car fumes, a whisky-run away. That's it. I'd run away to London. But first I had to walk past the boss, my replacement and, oh no, I had forgotten about him, the scout. Against great des-pair, bad times, humiliation, sadness or broken hearts, somehow dig-nity can rear its proud head. A wind of change can put those shoulders back, head up and eyes ahead, allowing no man to take the last grains of spirit away from you.

For a second I was about to copy Kevin Keegan's act for Liverpool in the Charity Shield match against Leeds United. Sent off with Billy Bremner, he removed his shirt and threw it at the bench. That gesture summed up his feelings toward the misappropriation of justice. The red shirt in the dust: a symbol of the individual's subjugation by a media-influenced decision which said he needed and deserved his comeuppance. But Keegan deserved to have himself and his perm dragged through the Wembley mud. His 'Yes Brian, well, thanks Brian' attitude off the pitch had overshadowed his actual playing abil-ity. This was the time when television had started to dominate the sport. A player's character could be distorted by a clever question from the interviewer like: 'Were you upset when they scored?' Or, 'Do you want to win the Cup?' That really probed, Brian.

Media technique was not and still isn't used by the big clubs. The players have been left to themselves. Warm lager, nob jokes and reading the *Beano* remain the mainstays of the professional footballer. Talking to the camera was left to the more adventurous types like Ian St John or Mick Channon.

'Ere I thought they were goot first 'alf 'n' n'so goot secon'.' 'The boys were brilliant. Great. Really brilliant, Ah think.' Lowbrow reporting is attractive to the British public. It guarantees you don't have to worry about anything. It takes responsibility away from the reader; participation ends when you buy a paper or watch the box. It ends there. Sit back and just soak it up.

The shirt was off my back. Instead of throwing it at the coach I placed it with great magnificence on the kit bag. I went up to the boss and said straight to his face, 'Stick yir team up yir arse.'

The heavens opened, sunlight fell on my head. Angels roared approval. On this note of pride I headed toward the dressing room. I observed I was being followed by the scout. He had witnessed this miscarriage of justice and obviously wanted to add a few points of his own like 'You were the best man on the park', or, 'How soon could you pack? You're going south.' Or even, 'You are the new Ron Yeats'. He approached me. My heart pounded. He tapped me on the shoulder. I turned. He said: 'Richard Jobson? I am arresting you on suspicion. . . .'

Blake Morrison

Blake is probably the only well-known poet to have been offered schoolboy terms by a top club, Preston North End. But he chose instead to go for a protracted academic career which ended in 1978 with a Ph.D. Having failed to become an academic he joined the Times Literary Supplement, *then the* Observer, *and is now literary editor of* The Independent on Sunday. *He has written children's books, criticism, and poetry, including* The Ballad of the Yorkshire Ripper.

Turf Moor,
and Other Fields of Dreams

BLAKE MORRISON

*5 kids still play at making blossoms fall
and humming as they do 'Here Comes the Bride'.
They never seem to tire of their ball
though I hear a woman's voice call one inside.*

*2 larking boys play bawdy bride and groom.
3 boys in Leeds strip la-la Lohengrin
I hear them as I go through growing gloom
still years away from being skald or skin.*

*The ground's carpeted with petals as I throw
the aerosol, the HARP can, the cleared weeds
on top of Dad's dead daffodils, then go,
with not one glance behind away from Leeds.*

'V', Tony Harrison

How they kept football from me for so long I don't know, but I was almost eleven before I discovered it – or should I say it discovered me. I remember the moment clearly. It was a Sunday morning in autumn and my father and I were sitting in adjoining armchairs in the dining room of our one-time rectory in Yorkshire, sunlight pouring in through the windows and over our shoulders. He had the *Sunday Times*, I the *Sunday Express*, and as I turned to the back page my eye fell on a photograph and match report. In an instant the wicked secret was out and I was doomed – another of the century's lost boys destined to squander the best years of his life failing to make the grade as a professional or simply supporting the wrong team.

Until that moment in the sunlight my only sporting interest had been motor racing: at Oulton Park and Aintree and Silverstone I'd seen Graham Hill and Jack Brabham, Roy Salvadori and Stirling Moss,

Bruce McLaren and Innes Ireland battle it out in Formula One races; at home with Dinky toys, I'd recreate these races in the back yard or round the legs of my father's billiard table. It wasn't much of a participation sport for a boy, and it's hard to imagine a child of the 1980s or 1990s finding anything exciting about a noisy, polluting, past-you-in-a-flash car race. But these were the years when the British dominated the sport, drivers as well as manufacturers, and the 1959 championship – with Jack Brabham pushing his car over the line in the final race to wrest victory from Stirling Moss and Tony Brooks – had all the last-gasp enthralment of the 1988-9 soccer season.

There were other dramas, too – like the system we devised for smuggling two large families into the Oulton Park paddock on a single ticket (slip it out to the next person through the slats of a wooden fence), or the extraordinary practice (when the last race was over) of being allowed to drive round the circuit in your family saloon.

Then on that day in 1961 I picked up the family paper and, looking for motor-racing news, saw instead a muddy goalmouth, a bulging net, and what the poet Vernon Scannell once called 'the blurred anguish of goalkeepers'. I pored over the match reports and league tables like someone trying to get to grips with a foreign language. And straight away, the grip was on me. Only once since, after that European Cup Final in the Heysel Stadium, when I thought I could never bear to play or watch the game again, has it promised to set me free.

My son, a child of the 1980s, got the soccer virus at seven. Surely I must have known about football before I was eleven? But there were just eighteen children at our village primary school, and football was not played there at all, not even in the playground.

At home it was no better. My father had never played football, only rugby, and as the local GP in an under-resourced practice was confined to home, on call, most weekends; when he wasn't, it was Oulton Park we'd go to, not a football ground. My cousins from Manchester, the only children I saw outside school, were all mad about car racing, too. Isolated as I was, the rich kid in the rectory, it wasn't so surprising that football hadn't impinged on my world. Like sex later, it was something my parents probably preferred me not to know about.

Yet eighteen miles away was the town of Burnley, not only my birthplace (in the district hospital) but home to one of the two great football teams of the day. By now, the point of my initiation, their greatest moment, when they won the 1959–60 championship, had already passed. But I was not to know that, and nor were any of the sports journalists who covered their games that autumn. Burnley were riding high, and even if they hadn't been it would never have occurred to me to support Leeds United, though the place we lived in was right on the Yorkshire–Lancashire border, almost as close to Elland Road as to Turf Moor. Who were Leeds United? Just some team languishing in a lower division. Whereas Burnley, as the autumn of 1961 gave way to the spring of 1962, looked on target for the double, and could boast a team of English, Irish and Scottish internationals: Blacklaw, Angus, Elder, Adamson, Cummings, Miller, Connelly, McIlroy, Pointer, Harris.

It was an exciting season but a sad one. The scrapbook I began, when I look at it more closely, reveals some odd gaps, and stops abruptly on 3 March, at which point Burnley were four points clear of Ipswich and five clear of Tottenham, with games in hand over both of them. (In the Second Division Liverpool made the pace ahead of Leyton Orient and Plymouth Argyle.) Thereafter, Burnley's progress was too agonizing to record, and I have suppressed all memory of it apart from a rare win over lowly Blackpool: inexorably, Ipswich caught us and the games in hand were blown away.

But there was still the FA Cup, the very reason, some commentators said (as they always do), for the team's faltering in the league. Here my scrapbook details are much fuller: 6–1 over QPR; then Leyton Orient, 1–0 in a replay; Everton, 3–1; Sheffield United 1–0; and finally in the semi-finals a 2–1 win over Fulham, again after a replay. This left the final against Spurs, the Old Enemy, who came to Turf Moor for a league match just fourteen days before and drew 2–2. There were four goals again at Wembley, but this time it all turned to dust. Jimmy Greaves scored after 3 minutes; Burnley's equalizer early in the second half came from Robson, who somehow squeezed it in the narrow gap that Brown was guarding at one post – anything but a classic. This goal was cancelled out by the burly Smith just 1 minute later.

Then came a disputed penalty 10 minutes from time: Blacklaw lost the ball to two challenging Spurs players (surely a foul), Cummings stepped in to breast away a shot by Merwin (never handball, ref) and the referee pointed to the spot. The decision was agony enough, but nothing compared to the slow-motion trauma of the penalty itself: tubby Adam Blacklaw dropping on one knee to his right as Danny Blanchflower stepped up and rolled the ball gently to his left. At the final whistle I did the only thing a boy could do in the circumstances: took my ball out on the front lawn and re-enacted the entire game, with certain crucial adjustments to the scoreline. This was the principle I'd learnt with my Dinky toys round the billiard table: a world of isolated make-believe, where the action replay, yet to be invented on television, ensured that your favourites could never lose. But to a growing boy there were shades of the prison house about these fantasy games: I wanted to play football myself, and that seemed to mean having somebody to play it with.

For the moment this possibility was remote. My younger sister soon tired of being put in goal and my long-suffering aunt Sheila, who came to stay every school holiday and who one summer allowed me to amass a century against her on the back lawn, would not extend her tolerance of cricket to football. As for the three boys of my age at primary school – Simon, Stephen, and Jeffrey – they were so uninterested in football they used to satirize my obsession with it. In desperation I started going to a youth club in Kelbrook, three miles away, where there was five-a-side every Friday evening and where the intention was to form a fully fledged eleven-a-side village boys' team. My grave offence to tribal loyalties somehow got back to Simon, Stephen and Jeffrey, who took the piss relentlessly – 'Morrie, Morrie, football mad' – and eventually stopped talking to me altogether. Their persecution programme only strengthened my faith: I was now a martyr to football, a sufferer in the cause.

Forced to play alone, I began the process of transforming some rough and gale-swept ground in the paddock behind our house into a stadium of dreams. My father helped me clear the ground of stones, weeds, broken glass. We constructed goal posts from rusty old metal tubing and put some strawberry nets behind them. (To my dad's fury I left the nets there the whole winter until grass and weed began to grow through and they fell apart in our hands.) The touchlines were ribbon-scatters of sawdust, standard local league practice in those days. But one afternoon I discovered an old line-marker and some lime bags in an outhouse, from the days when the house had a tennis court. Clearing the cobwebs, I slowly grasped how the contraption worked:

you poured lime into the heavy metal base, added water, stirred the sloppy mass with a stick until you had the right consistency, dropped the wheel into the metal slots that held it, and then went squeaking off down the side of the pitch.

In Kevin Costner's 1989 film *Field Of Dreams*, an American on a farm hears the corn telling him to construct a baseball field at the back of his house. I had the same sense of mystery and religious calling myself, though for this Yorkshire field of dreams it was that line-marker which provided all the magic. The touchlines and penalty areas and centre circle would be a pale, indistinguishable yellow when I marked them out on the wet grass in the morning; by lunchtime, as the day dried out, they'd come up a brilliant white. I surveyed them from the main stand – a large earth mound running down one side of the field, separating it from our garden. It was a short pitch, thirty yards at most, and a bumpy one, narrower at one end than the other and with a ridge running across the edge of the penalty areas. But as far as I was concerned – little Lord Fauntleroy on his earth mound, chairman, groundsman, manager, and twenty-two players rolled into one – these were the green expanses of Turf Moor or even Wembley.

I lacked only opponents, but these weren't hard to imagine, anymore than it was hard to provide Ken Wolstenholme's commentary as I raced up and down. My favourite move was to pass back to myself in goal, then punt the ball high in the air and sprint up to the centre circle to head forward; a further rush, a volley on the edge of the area and with luck the ball might hit the roof of the net without bringing down the wonky crossbar as well. (Why was it always so much more exciting to hit the roof of the net, though all the manuals said that a low shot stood more chance of beating the keeper? Why is that sort of goal still so much more spectacular to see?) A line of elms and chestnuts ran down the side of the pitch opposite the grandstand, a kop that roared and swayed in the wind: if I timed it right there'd be a gust of wind at just the moment the strawberry net was bulging – the ecstatic crowd, or even Ken Wolstenholme moved to excitement by what had happened.

It was all very well but I'd have to put in some proper games of football – with real opponents – if I was ever going to be signed up by Burnley. Then one spring evening as I was dashing about the pitch and muttering Wolstenholmeisms to myself, Simon and Stephen were

127

suddenly there at the field gate. I slunk over to them, shamefaced, caught in the act, only to find that they'd decided they liked football and, more to the point, had resolved to persecute Jeffrey instead. Things looked up after that, for me if not for Jeffrey; we started to play football at break and even managed to con the soppy new teacher at the primary school into letting us have a match during lesson time.

The Kelbrook team got off the ground, too, if only for two matches, one of which exposed me for the first time to violence (unthinkable in our school for a boy to be beaten up by another boy) and the other to the four-letter word 'f - - -': it was in the bath afterwards, I remember, that I half-innocently asked my mother what the word meant and knew from her fumbling evasiveness that it possessed a power I would want to test out again. Football and f - - - ing (whatever that was) were, I intuitively grasped, a long way from my mother's aspirations for me, which among other things included learning to play the piano. I dutifully went to piano lessons at the house of Mrs Brown, in Earby, until I arrived one Wednesday afternoon in the middle of live television coverage (rare in those days) of an England World Cup qualifying match. To have the football on television turned off and to be forced to practise the piano instead put paid to my faltering interest in that instrument. I have never been musical since.

Later, in September 1962, I moved on to a grammar school in Skipton and at last found boys even more manacled to football than myself. Undeterred that rugby, not soccer, was the official school sport, we would get to the playing fields early on games afternoons so we could use the oval ball as a round one (even heading in) before the games master arrived. And though soccer was in theory banned from the playground, the staff were happy to turn a blind eye to our break-time mauling outside the art room: there was a chalked goal on one wall, but to score at the other end you had to get the ball between the drainpipe and the ventilation-grate. Mostly we played with a tennis ball but if there wasn't one to be had we'd make do with a small stone instead. (Out walking at thirty-nine, I still find myself trying to steer small stones through gateposts or other imaginary goals.) For a time we even got away with using a Frido. It all ended the morning I sent a wayward shot towards a doorway at exactly the moment that Harry Evans, the notoriously fierce physics master, came whistling through it on his way to assembly. Like the Blanchflower penalty, I see it all now in horrible slow motion: his unexpected emergence; the Frido smacking him on his bald patch and leaving a neat imprint of mud dots across his forehead; his terrifyingly loud demand 'Who kicked that?'; me shuffling over in terror and contrition as he began to wipe the muddy print off with his handkerchief; an almost audible general sigh of relief that punishment went no further than confisca-tion of the ball and detention for all those of us who'd been playing. For half a term there was no playground football at all. Then the tennis ball games resumed.

Playing regular rugby for the school would have made it difficult to pursue a soccer career, of course, but whether through design or lack of skill I rose no higher than captaincy of the third XV, where I played stand-off (lots of kicking, not much service to the three-quarters) and took all the penalties. This left nearly all my Saturdays free to go to Burnley and, later, to play for a team in Colne; only once was I caught out, when I had to bunk off from a third XV game in order to play in a crucial cup match at Lancaster, which we won 5–3 in a swirling wind that allowed me, for the only time in my career, to score direct from a corner.

Sundays were reserved for the phenomenally successful Barnoldswich Park Rovers Minor Side, which I joined at fifteen, just after the start of a season which ended with a long unbeaten run and the league title. I didn't think of myself as much of a player but both schoolyard practice and the solitary hours I spent at home modelling myself on Burnley midfield genius Gordon Harris did mean that I was highly trained and motivated. And there was one spectacular goal which helped me make my mark, at least as far as the local paper was concerned. ('Left winger Laurence Stocker raced away down the right wing before putting across a bullet-like centre. Blake Morrison, who had followed up field, came running in to head the ball into the corner of the net with the entire Hellifield defence left stranded': I still don't know if I meant it or just could not get out of the way.)

The team went on winning the following season, and soon there were rumours of scouts coming to Barlick in order to watch us: Liver-pool, Leeds United, Burnley, Bury and Blackburn were all said to be 'taking an interest' and Preston manager Jimmy Milne himself turned up for one game. Finally an invitation came for six of us to go to Pres-ton for trials. The local paper made much of the fact that I was among them, a grammar-school boy and doctor's son, but we all knew that it was the other grammar-school boy among the six, Seehan Grace, three years younger than most of us and a star sprinter, whom Preston must be after. Nonetheless, after two lots of trials, three of us were offered schoolboy forms.

It seems amazing now that we were so blasé as to refuse, but we were taking the advice of our mentors – Park Rovers stalwarts like Neville Thwaites and Teddy Bamber as well as Seehan Grace's dad, who ran the Barlick carpet shop and knew the score better than we did. Their view was that schoolboy forms wouldn't mean much – no more than a couple of games a season in the B-team. And though I was tempted to give it a go just to see what the level of competition was like, I didn't want to break ranks. Preston, in any case, were not Burnley. O-levels were looming, I'd begun to get interested in girls and poetry, and deep down I knew I'd neither the skill nor bottle to make a soccer career.

Still, I went on playing. Langroyd, the Colne adult side I played for on Saturdays, had a lousy sloping pitch and were no great shakes, but I was enough of a fantasist to persuade myself that the stocky young apprentice engineers and flabby, middle-aged mill workers who made up the rest of the team were in the same league as Gordon Harris and Ray Pointer.

We had a fantasist for a manager, too. Ernie, who had been a good player in his day and still sometimes turned out if we were one short, lived in a grim terrace in Earby with an outsize wife and mentally disabled teenage daughter. Football was his escape from the pressures at home, and he was even more obsessed with it than I was. Unfortunately, he was also a cheat, and had a habit of drafting in star players for one-off appearances in cup matches even if this meant forging their signing-on forms. He got away with it most of the time but there were two notable occasions when his cheating caught up with us. The first was a summer five-a-side tournament, when the Langroyd A-team were progressing steadily towards the final until, in the semi, 1–0 up with 5 minutes to go, one of our players went down injured. We didn't have a substitute and didn't reckon we needed one either but Ernie, taking no risks, illegally sent on someone from our B-team, an offence immediately spotted by a rival team manager, who reported it and had us disqualified.

Easier to forgive, in some ways, was Ernie's ploy when we found ourselves 1–0 down at half-time in a crucial quarter-final cup match in Skelmersdale: Langroyd had been beaten in the final the previous year, and we were determined to triumph this time. The game should never have started on the waterlogged pitch, and the rain continued to bucket down. Skelmersdale got a squelchy early goal and there was worse to come when our centre half was sent off after 20 minutes for taking a wild kick at a niggly opposition forward. In the dressing room at the interval Ernie told us – and none of us disputed it – that since we'd hardly got out of our own penalty area there was no chance of our winning; the best thing would be for a succession of players to go down injured and be taken off, forcing the referee to recognize the error of his ways in not having called the game off. I couldn't bring myself to be one of the imposters, but there were a couple of players who made a brilliant job of shamming serious injury and when the second of these had been helped off, after 72 minutes, leaving us with eight men, the referee decided to abandon the match – the pitch, he said, with no exaggeration, was now unplayable. Judging by the whistling from the Skelmersdale stand, the crowd had clearly got Ernie's number: we were even booed as we left the ground for the team coach at the end. But Skelmersdale had the last laugh, invoking some arcane Lancashire League rule that if a game had been abandoned after 70 minutes the authorities had the right to allow the result to stand. Ernie was phoneless and it fell to me to ring the appeals committee to learn the result of their hearing, and to drive down to Ernie to break the bad news. I remember him, in his cramped front room full of ironing and football trophies, his nylon shirt covered in sweat, indignantly planning our next move. But there was none we could make: Langroyd were out of the cup, and my last season with them before I left for university was all but over.

My interest in Burnley was all but over, too. I had gone on watching them throughout the 1960s, but they were in steady decline and my memories of the period are random and fragmented. I saw newly promoted Liverpool come up to Turf Moor and win 3–0 with Ian St John thumping one goal straight up into the roof of the net from about 2 yards; I remember an Aston Villa defender squaring up to Willie Irvine (or was it another of Burnley's flash-in-the-pan forwards of that era?) then nutting him full in the face: we howled for his blood, a linesman had spotted it, and off he went. Clearest of all – I remember it as yesterday – there was the most spectacular own goal ever seen at Turf Moor, scored for Leeds United (just up from the Second Division) by Alex Elder, who won the ball near his own corner flag, brought it forward a yard or two then, without looking, lofted it back to Adam Blacklaw. But Blacklaw had advanced towards the edge of the penalty area, and would have had no chance anyway with Elder's overhit lob, which swung into the far top corner. The only goal in a 1–0 defeat by Leeds: things were never the same after that.

There were still the odd moments of glory, but not many. The last programme I have is against Arsenal – from 13 September 1969, two weeks before I left for university. Arsenal that day had Bob Wilson in goal, plus Frank McLintock, Bobby Gould and George Graham; the Burnley team was Peter Mellor, John Angus, Les Latcham, Brian O'Neil, Dave Merrington, Sammy Todd, Dave Thomas, Ralph Coates, Frank Casper, Martin Dobson and Steve Kindon. It was still a classy outfit – or should have been with Dobson, O'Neil and Coates there – but only Angus was left from the Cup Final side seven years earlier and the inexorable slide had begun. Two seasons later, in 1971, Burnley were relegated. They quickly climbed back up again, but only for two seasons, and then cascaded down until they reached the Fourth Division in 1985. In 1988 they escaped plummeting out of the Football League altogether by winning their last match: I heard it on the radio from a Suffolk garden, urging them on as if I were back on the terraces and this were a Cup Final, not a battle for survival.

Already by the end of the 1960s the crowds at Turf Moor had begun to peter out. In those days I went with Les, a manager at the Barlick Rolls Royce factory, and we'd park his warm, purring saloon a couple of streets away, before taking our place on the empty terraces or in the stand. But in the early 1960s I had travelled to matches with a carpenter named Geoff, in his battered old van, and we'd have to park miles away from the ground and walk; once inside, we'd stand behind the goal where the crowds were sometimes big enough for me to experience that feeling of being carried helplessly downwards, feet off the ground, after some particularly exciting goalmouth incident.

Intimidation, violence and vandalism we took for granted. Whenever I'm tempted to look back on that decade as some innocent age of pre-hooliganism, I remember my brush with a Stoke City fan when I was about thirteen. He was walking ahead of me as (in those unsegregated days) I looked for a place behind the goal. Catching sight of my claret and blue scarf, he abruptly stopped and wouldn't budge, so that when I gingerly tried to make my way past his looming bulk he could turn and snarl: 'Who the f - - - do you think you're pushing?' He grabbed hold of me, dangled me in the air in front of him, drew his fist back and was about to belt me when a mate of his called him off: 'Leave 'im Mick, it's not worth it, he's nobbut a little 'un.' He put me down: 'Just f - - - - - - watch it next time.'

Violence had its own momentum and needed no excuses. I remember the story of a friend beaten up in Skipton bus station. 'Hey, you're t' c - - - what's been cleverin' roun' town all evenin'.'

'Nay, ah've been in Keighley – ah've just got off t'bus.'

'That's nowt to wi' it.' Thump.

At the Heysel stadium, and again after Hillsborough last year, I wondered whether the violence and tragedy that attend football might not kill off the pleasure I've always taken in it. But there's no sign of that. On the contrary, with my young son's fantasies to look after as well as my own, I've renewed my interest. That interest began as a kind of vicarious dream, and it still operates on that level. Listening to Burnley's great escape act the other season, I wasn't thinking how fortunate I was not to be there, squalidly ending my playing days at the bottom of the Fourth Division. I was wondering why the call from the Burnley manager hadn't come yet, and staying fairly close to the phone in case it did.

Antony Easthope

Antony came to Manchester – and football – relatively late in life, in 1969. For him the game merged with his political and social ideas. After going to Cambridge on a scholarship in the late 1950s he travelled extensively before taking up teaching English at Manchester Polytechnic, where he is now a senior lecturer. Married with three children, he is the author of four books, including What a Man's Gotta Do – the Masculine Myth in Popular Culture.

Manchester United and the Miners' Strike

ANTONY EASTHOPE

There's a hell of a lot of politics in football. I don't think Henry Kissinger would have lasted forty-eight hours at Old Trafford.

Tommy Docherty

As far as football is concerned I was a late developer. I didn't take the game seriously until my thirties when I came to teach in Manchester. Then there was only one club – Manchester United from 1970 to 1977, the end of the old Law, Best and Charlton team, and the coming of Tommy Docherty's young side of 1975–7. From this great team I learned at last to appreciate association football. But for me it was more than that. Following Docherty's Red Army was part of my education in the passions of the north of England and the potential of class politics.

I was born in Portsmouth – and you cannot get much further south than that – at just the time Mr Hitler's bombers came across the channel to try and kill me. But I was brought up in south London, in the endless and soulless mock-Tudor suburbs that stretch to the horizon round Kingston, a zone which was something of a cultural desert for football. Some would argue that the emergence of Wimbledon has not altered this.

In those days the nearest First Division team played twenty miles north across the river in Fulham, while Crystal Palace pursued its lonely fortunes the same distance away to the east. The local team, Kingstonian, if I recall correctly, weren't even in the Third Division (South). On top of this early cultural deprivation, I passed the eleven-plus and went to a socially aspirant grammar school which in the dull 1950s was determined to pass itself off as Harrow. This meant an obsession with every sport so long as it wasn't soccer. Rugby was compulsory twice a week for all boys who did not have a documented medical certificate. To be honest, at the time I loved it.

In 1968 someone persuaded me to watch the European Cup Final when, of course, Manchester United beat Benfica 4–1, and I felt a strange tingle, rather like a ten-year-old's idea of sex. But this was mere football foreplay, for in 1969 I got a job in Manchester. For me this was a foreign country – as a south Londoner the north at that point had meant going to parties in Hampstead. Somehow I couldn't believe the prison was called Strangeways or the graveyard was called Waste Cemetery. I started to go to football with some fellow teachers: Emrys who supported Liverpool, and Dave, a miner's son, estranged Yorkshireman and Leeds United follower. Our tastes were catholic and we went wherever there was a good game. For my innocent southern eyes – and ears – the experience had all the magic found only by a recent convert; not only the game itself and the northern intimacy and intensity, but the fact of coming across 'the people'.

We went to Liverpool, along the grim motorway over Chat Moss to Anfield Road. When a well-known bald referee came out to start the game he was greeted with the universal chant of 'Kojak, Kojak'. On the Saturday after Ian St John got his OBE he was on the receiving end of a tackle from Norman Hunter so harsh it silenced the crowd until a lone voice cried out, 'Hit him with yer medal'. During the early 1970s we always seemed to be there when Leeds United sneaked an early goal against the run of play and then, with Revie's unique blend of flint and skill, held it until the final whistle. We always went on the Kop and it didn't matter at all if Dave cheered for Leeds – no one believed him.

We went to Maine Road, where unlike the Kop you could stand on your own two feet and didn't need to worry so much about someone peeing in your pocket, to watch Mike Summerbee, Francis Lee and that supreme athlete, Colin Bell. In 1972 Manchester City were a good team, and might have repeated their 1968 success and won the League Championship again. In March, Peter Swales, who has known little success in football but happens to control the club, decided to buy Rodney Marsh from Queens Park Rangers. Marsh's particular brand of cockney individualism unbalanced and undermined the whole team, which doesn't appear to have ever recovered.

Football belongs to the supporters, or should do. They make it happen; it's their gate money which pays for the players' wages, and the toilet paper in the changing rooms and, to be sure, the directors' Havana cigars. Never forget, their unfailing support prompts the advertisers and sponsors to invest millions in football. So why shouldn't fans have some control over their team, possibly through the supporters clubs? In fact, grounds, facilities and players are owned by a board of directors, giving them the legal right to do what they want: to dismiss managers as they choose, buy and sell players at a whim. There were many people on the terraces at Maine Road who would never have voted for City to buy the Loftus Road whizz kid. Yet, he did have his followers. 'Rodney Marsh is King' is still scrawled outside our local Tesco, inscrutable to anyone born after 1960. Swales and Marsh not withstanding, we were in the middle of the Kippax in 1974 when City played Liverpool and won 2–0 with an amazing four-move goal started by Bell, who then sprinted 50 yards to lay it on for Dennis Tueart to finish. My friend Emrys, who is a big lad, continued to shout on Liverpool to the end despite standing next to an even larger City fan who was very big indeed. After Bell's goal this man-mountain turned to Emrys, lifted him up by his elbows, kissed him once on each cheek, and gently put him back in his place again. We were all very quiet after that.

And of course we went to Old Trafford, my real football home. However good it was at Elland Road, Maine Road or Anfield, Old Trafford was a move to a higher plane, especially if we had queued for two hours to get into a key match or the derby game. I watched George Best on many occasions, and he *was* the most wildly gifted player of his generation. But what I shall never forget is the match against Liverpool in 1972. The Liverpool fullback, whose identity I shall omit in the name of decency, was known as a bit of a hard man and, incidentally, a drinker. He had clearly been told to hit Best early and hit him often, which he did, right down in front of us. Yet Best didn't once retaliate, but simply peeled himself up off the turf with a stoical smile, like Tom after being run over by a steamroller in the cartoons. Frail as he looked, he was one of the strongest players ever, as well as the most brilliant.

After Busby left, the owners didn't know what to do and started unnervingly hiring and firing managers, none of whom really had the confidence to cut and rebuild the team completely. From 1970 to 1974 it lived on the memory of its former glory, but the underlying trend was down, down, down. Even so, sometimes Charlton, Law and of course Best could combine and pull out the old inspiration, and one of those occasions came in 1971. Sheffield United had just been promoted and were taking the First Division by storm. On a dazzlingly bright and warm autumn day before a crowd of 63,000 the old United took them apart, 2–0, and went top of the division. That day all the clichés came alive – the stadium was a cauldron, the crowd was fused together in a single sustained high passion that increased after each goal. The promise that 'You'll never walk alone' seemed real.

Occasions like this made football a new class experience for me. Growing up in the London suburbs and going to a grammar school, I picked up the middle-class prejudice that any unofficial assembly of working-class people was a mindless, fascist mob. This is a prejudice television constantly reinforces in the way it selects and records almost any mass action – strikes, pickets, marches, demonstrations, football crowds. It always looks at them with only one question in mind: when will the violence begin? Standing on the terraces I found something I'd never known before. There were moments of aggression but I remember more the agony and ecstacy, when the adrenalin went through you so fast it made you quiver, a feeling made ten times stronger because it was shared at the same time with 40,000 other people cupped by the stands. Such rare moments conceal a very different sense of unity, made up of dogged commitment, abrasive comic humour, intelligent criticism and an almost bottomless fatalism.

During the 1960s I'd been a libertarian, believing that no mere social obligation or archaic laws should stop an individual pursuing happiness in their own brain or with any other part of the body. That was fine then, and it carried me far through the decade. Moving to Manchester and into the 1970s, I discovered it would take more than libertarianism to achieve human happiness. It became clear that the obstacles to self-fulfilment were much more solid than a few bad laws; they were in fact the institutions of present society which served the interests of a ruling class. Parliamentary democracy is fine as far as it goes, but it only does for the weekend – it ignores the place a person works from Monday to Friday. Owners and managers hold completely undemocratic power over the people who work for them and who have never voted for them in their lives. Democracy, if we believe in it, has got to extend through all life. Support for it has to be massive and organized and can only come from the working class as a whole. Where could you see that class and its power if it wasn't represented by the crowds streaming into Old Trafford? Or, as it happened, by the miners.

In 1974 the unthinkable happened. Time finally ran out for the old Manchester United side and they were relegated, at Old Trafford, by Manchester City, with a delicate penalty area back heel from Denis Law. However, with Tommy Docherty as the new manager, United swapped George Best, and memories, for youth and a new vision. They began winning steadily in the Second Division, and beat a lot of established First Division teams in an extended Cup run, which was followed by promotion. The graffiti round Manchester named them as 'Doc's Red Army'.

At the same time another Red Army was on the move. The miners' demand for a pay rise was refused by the Conservative government in October 1973 and an overtime ban started to put the lights out by Christmas, leading to the three-day week in the New Year. The NUM voted for an all-out strike on 4 February, and groups of miners toured up and down the country to power stations and docks to try to get workers there to stop using coal. Invariably they were supported, so strong was the feeling in their favour. With the country at a standstill, Ted Heath called a General Election over the question 'Who Governs Britain?', thus at a stroke achieving what the Left had been trying to do since Chartism: turn a massively popular industrial dispute into a Parliamentary political issue. Labour won the election.

From January 1974 to the summer of 1975 was an extraordinary political time for Britain. There was an unprecedented alliance between a radical Parliamentary programme, with the 'Alternative Economic Strategy', and Tony Benn as Minister for Industry and widespread, mobilized popular support. In my eyes, and not just mine, the crowds gathering each Saturday at the Stretford End had the solidarity and militancy of revolutionary masses. If only they could be motivated and led as the miners had been. These days, this might sound somewhat naive, but remember it was an era when Labour won elections and radicalism was far more prevalent. The Right were still, just, on the retreat, and a revolutionary Red Army was a permissible theory.

Through the winter of 1975 and the spring of 1976, the eleven representatives of the other Red Army were playing like no one else. Martin Buchan, Brian Greenhoff, Lou Macari, Gerry Daly, Steve Coppell, Gordon Hill, Sammy McIlroy, Stuart Pearson and the rest, Docherty's United were not just individual heroes but a very young, very beautiful team. With four in defence and four forwards, including Coppell and Hill as out and out wingers, they left just Macari and Daly in midfield, and had to play beyond themselves in a high risk strategy. This golden United were weak in defence, perhaps, but otherwise, Attack! Attack! Attack! - short quick passes, always going forward. As we used to say at the time, if they got two, okay we'd get three, and it happened like that often enough for the United cavalry to finish third in the league in 1976. But they also made it to the FA Cup Final, which they lost to Southampton by a single, lucky goal. Half the team came off in tears and made no secret of it, they were that young. But their time would come, unlike the miners.

Elsewhere, the British working class were also suffering defeat. The General Election had been won by a right-wing Labour Party, and Harold Wilson spent the next twelve months defusing the radical energies released by the crisis. By June 1975, he was strong enough to move Benn from Industry to the much less influential job as Minister for Energy. The process of weakening the party's commitment to a socialist programme accelerated, and in 1976 the economy had to be bailed out by the international bankers with the usual price to be paid in deflationary policies, cuts in government expenditure, wage restraint, and a rise in unemployment. For British politics the 1980s really began in 1976.

In the 1976-7 season, United came sixth in the league, but their moment came in the Cup Final on 21 May when they beat Liverpool 2-1. Four days later, Liverpool, who had already won the league, took the European Cup, beating Borussia Mönchengladbach 3-1. After the game I 'phoned Emrys to congratulate Liverpool on proving themselves the second-best team in Europe. On the Sunday after the Wembley Final when United rode back into Manchester in triumph crowds lined the streets far out into Cheshire, and when the bus finally reached the city centre in the late evening, nearly a million people waving red flags and scarves spilled over from Albert Square and down Peter Street, where the infamous Peterloo Massacre took place in 1819. We took over the whole city and could have had the factories, the offices, the police stations and Granada TV for the asking. But we didn't. After the players disappeared inside the Town Hall everybody went quietly home leaving the city – and the political arena – empty for Maggie Thatcher to do whatever she wanted.

The policies of Thatcherism had effectively started with Harold Wilson's Labour Government, and in 1977 the Ridley Committee was already meeting to defeat the miners next time around, although they didn't get their chance until 1984. Meanwhile at Old Trafford the power of the bosses was reasserted. In the summer of 1977 the owners fired Tommy Docherty on the grounds that he was having an affair with the physio's wife. (If every manager got fired for adultery there'd not be many left to run the game.) So it was obviously a pretext for getting rid of the Doc, whose aggressive, proletarian style they never liked. The team he had built was broken up.

I married and settled down in Manchester, and my kids grew up there thinking I still talk with a foreign accent. When they were old enough I took them with me to Maine Road, because I didn't fancy taking kids to Old Trafford. We stood in the rain for two hours in a badly policed crowd, the kids had to go fifty yards to use filthy, stinking toilets, City lost, and the whole thing, with programmes, slimy hot dogs and Bovril cost me nearly twenty quid. Neither I nor they wanted to repeat the experience. I don't go to matches any more. I sometimes watch the American football on Channel 4, though on Sunday mornings I do catch myself going down the results and league tables.

On reflection, I now see the politics of football differently. In the Victorian period, as has been said, religion was the opium of the people and Methodism saved the country from revolution. With the decline of religious faith, the old enthusiasms have been diverted into football. It gives the equivalent passions of ecstasy and despair, and promises the same feeling of righteous justification if your local team wins national honours, and even the Queen smiles in recognition. In real life those born rich have an unfair advantage from the start, but on the football field, as presumably in Heaven, everybody is given an equal chance to show their individual talents.

The peoples' game does not encourage working-class activism – it's a substitute for it.

Roy Hattersley

A Sheffield Wednesday supporter who follows them – home and away – whenever time permits, Roy is a journalist and author, and is also trying to bring down Mrs Thatcher's Government, as deputy leader of the Labour Party. His great football moments were playing for Sheffield City Grammar School and a Wednesday victory over Tottenham's Double team of the early 1960s. He became MP for Birmingham Sparkbrook in 1964 at the age of thirty.

Wednesday at the Weekend

ROY HATTERSLEY

The football fan is not just a watcher. His sweat and his nerves work on football, and his spirit can be made rich or destitute by it.

Arthur Hopcraft, *The Football Man*

It was love at first sight. The war was not quite over and real league football was still the promise of next year. But Sheffield Wednesday were at home to Nottingham Forest and Nottingham Forest was my father's team. In our house all the difficult decisions were taken by my mother. So I suppose it was she who decided that I was old enough and big enough to push my own way through the juvenile turnstile: it is inconceivable that my father shepherded me through with him and paid the full admission price for a boy of ten. I cannot recall, but I can easily imagine my father's anxiety as he waited for me to join him inside the ground. If I had been lost or damaged it would have been his responsibility and I would not have been allowed to go with him to football for another five years.

He was used to company at matches. Before the war, he and his two young brothers never missed a game. At first they stood outside the ground until half-time, when the gates were opened and the unemployed were let in free. For years they enjoyed that special football pleasure of the close companion to whom no comment – however banal or biased – would cause embarrassment. With his brothers away, I was expected to assume their mantle. And so I did for over two decades. And now, after almost as long without him, I still miss his presence at my shoulder – eating Mintoes and watching the papers pile up at his feet and telling the stories that had been told at football matches since he was a boy. No ball ever flew in the air without him reminding me of an adage in some ancient Nottinghamshire newspaper.

'Only angels play up there,' he used to say.

I always laughed, partly out of love and loyalty and partly because it hid all my anxieties.

Anxiety became a regular part of my Saturday afternoons from that first Saturday onwards when I went with my father to Hillsborough because Nottingham Forest were his team. Wednesday have been mine ever since. Cynics will say that, because of that, my anxiety has been wholly justified. The story is more complicated than they know.

We sat in the old stands until I was thirteen. Then I was adjudged capable of enduring the rigours of the Spion Kop. For the next five years I played football in the mornings – under-14s, second XI and then the full glory of the Sheffield City Grammar School itself. The morning game created my first anxiety – I was worried about my own result, then about my own performance. Next my worry was getting from the school ground to Hillsborough. My father's was the constant fear that I would cause trouble. I was a peaceable, not to say timid boy except when wearing football boots and anyway in those days rival fans stood side by side on the same terraces and rarely exchanged an aggressive word. But father always believed that I would start some sort of riot.

In half a decade only one problem ever occurred. A boy – not a footballer but a classmate – accompanied us to the match. To my father's embarrassed astonishment, when it started to rain he put up an umbrella. The boy was called Peter Middleton. As the umbrella should have warned us, he went into the Civil Service. He is now Permanent Secretary to the Treasury.

My father's rules about the Spion Kop – also the product of his anxiety – were absolute and unnegotiable. We stood in front, not behind, a barrier. After a hard morning of shoulder charges and sliding tackles, I wanted to lean on the steel rail. But I was always required to keep the stanchion in the small of my back and was not allowed to put my hands in my pockets, so that when the crowd peered down to get a better view of a corner or penalty I would be prepared to protect myself against the pushing, tripping and other sorts of mayhem. My father would have expected the protection – had it been necessary – to involve minimum force, but he was in a perpetual state of terror that one day he would take me home with a black eye and have to answer for it to my mother.

We never left the ground until quarter past five. Had I thought that we remained in order to avoid the crush I would have felt cossetted and embarrassed. But we stayed on for wholly honourable reasons. Some time after five o'clock, results from other matches were relayed to the waiting crowd by the ancient expedient of displaying boards which signified the full-time scores. Each score was hung under an identifying letter. As we compared the letters to the fixture lists on the back of our programme, my father always claimed that he was making a rough check of his pools coupon, before its careful comparison with the Green 'Un later that night. In fact I knew that he was waiting to see if Nottingham Forest had won. These days, on the rare, unhappy occasions that I cannot watch the Wednesday, I still wait until somebody tells me the scores. There is only one result which really matters.

Waiting for Wednesday's result – whether I am there in person, counting off the last seconds (when we lead by one goal) or on some distant ground waiting to hear vital news – is only one of the anxieties that still surrounds my Saturdays. It is the most reasonable of all my apprehensions. For back in the early 1950s, when I stood on the red shale of the old Spion Kop, Wednesday were promoted one year and relegated the next with a frequency that earned them the nickname of the Yo-Yo team. And these days, when I watch in greater luxury, they seem to approach each April on the verge of relegation back to the Second Division. Not to worry about them would be treachery. But some of my other concerns are less rational.

For forty years I have approached the Sheffield Wednesday ground neurotically afraid that I will arrive just as the gates are being locked on a capacity crowd or so late that I will be exiled to some other corner of the terraces where it is impossible to see either goal or the centre spot. It is now a wholly unreasonable neurosis. For I arrive at half past two, leave my car in a designated car park bay and sit in the warm comfort of the directors' box. But the agony remains. As I drive slowly north from the city centre, the floodlight pylons come to view above the factories and terraced houses, and I begin to panic that the gates will be closed and bolted. On rainy days that fear takes over some time after two o'clock: for the previous five hours, if there has been the lightest of showers, I concentrate all my paranoia on the fear that the ground will be waterlogged and the match abandoned.

The fear of finding the ground already full dates back to my formative years as a football enthusiast and Wednesday suppporter. My obsessive affection was developed during the years when capacity crowds were commonplace. That was during the time when I was playing football in the mornings and between full-time in my own game and kick-off at Hillsborough had to travel by bus from the playing fields of remote Derbyshire schools or by two tramcars from the Gleadless ground of the City Grammar School. There was also a problem about what to do with an old army haversack stuffed with muddy boots, wet shirt and bedraggled shorts. Only once was I so late that the turnstiles were about to close. And even then I managed to slip through. My father was waiting faithfully on the other side of the boundary wall and we stood together, so high on the Spion Kop that there were dock plants and daisies under our feet. Oscar Fox scored the winning goal against Blackpool. But we did not see it. My father, being a gentle man, forgave me.

In those days Hillsborough hosted a semi-final every year. That was a chance to watch football rather than worry about the result and it was an opportunity which I always took despite the difficulty of enjoying the privilege of watching Newcastle United on their way to two Cup victories and the joys of seeing the great teams which played in Derby County, Wolverhampton Wanderers and Manchester United colours in the years that followed the war. Tickets used to go on sale at ten o'clock on the previous Sunday. My father and I took our places in an already substantial queue at a little after six. Normally we had achieved our heart's desire by about half past eleven and were home in time to hear the beginning of 'Family Favourites' at noon. On the day of the match – fortunately during the Easter holidays when I had no game to play – we arrived at the ground a good three hours before the kick-off and were in our places (in front of the barrier and with hands free from pockets) more than ninety minutes before the match began. We thus spent six times as long preparing to watch the game as we actually spent watching it. Not for a moment did either of us think that the time was wasted.

For me, however, those semi-finals did not compare with Wednesday games. For the true supporter is not interested in the quality of the game but in the result. Only that prejudiced passion allows for the fantasies which are essential to the little boy's enjoyment. And it is that early obsession which ensures that middle-aged men remain faithful to a team which, as long as they have breath in their bodies, will never walk alone. I have grown out of wilder imaginings. I no longer strain to listen to each announcement over the crackling tannoy in case the broadcast should say 'Will Roy Hattersley come to the players' entrance at once and bring his boots with him?'

Nor do I still believe in the super fan who refused to eat streaky bacon because its red and white stripes reminded him of Sheffield United. But I still wholly identify with the team and its supporters. When I get to heaven and I am asked about my proudest moment, I know what the answer will be. Returning from Manchester to Sheffield a fellow Wednesdayite asked me the most complimentary of questions.

'We know which team you support, but which party do you belong to?' There are problems about being the oldest and possibly the most respectable of all Sheffield Wednesday's travelling supporters. In 1980, the year of promotion from the Third Division, I arrived at Oxford without having arranged a ticket. The stand was full and obediently I made my way to the terrace which is designated to 'Away Supporters'. A steward stood in front of the steel gate. He looked at my dark blue overcoat, noticed that I was wearing gloves and offered his considered opinion.

'You don't want to go in there. "They" are in there.' I told him that I was one of 'them' and, with some reluctance, he unlocked the gate and holding it just wide enough for me to squeeze inside told me that he took no responsibility for my safety and welfare.

It was an exceptional afternoon. Sheffield Wednesday won 3–1 and began their slow progress towards promotion and the Second Division. Almost as important I was approached by a Wednesday supporter who was a caricature of all that travelling fans are supposed to be. He wore hobnailed boots and tattered jeans and a sleeveless pullover which was not reinforced by a shirt. Down one arm was tattooed the word 'Jackie' and down the other 'Charlton'. When he waved his clenched fist – a regular part of the afternoon's pleasure – I noticed that 'hate' was engraved on one set of knuckles and 'love' on the other. A Sheffield Wednesday scarf was tied to each wrist and another draped round his neck. His crew-cut had a blue and white stripe running where the parting should have been.

I managed to avoid him until the game was over, but then having offered a victory embrace to everyone else within arm's reach he turned to me.

'Are you called Hattersley?' Nervously I admitted it. 'Did I,' he demanded, 'hear you on the radio last week?' I pleaded guilty for a second time.

'And did you say that you supported Sheffield Wednesday?' I told him that he was correct again. Grasping me in a bearhug he shouted over my shoulder as he bent my spine.

'I'm proud to meet you. It takes a real man to admit to supporting Wednesday.'

It takes a real man – and a substantial woman – to be an away supporter of any team these days. Identifying as I do with the other fans, I spend late Saturday afternoons in a constant agony of guilt about the way in which they are treated. For a couple of years, I refused to go to Luton at all on the basis that if other Wednesday supporters were not allowed in the ground there was no room for me. Then the Wednesday needed a point and they looked like triumphing even on the artificial pitch. So I turned up to urge them on in their fight against relegation.

When the police announce the visitors are to be kept locked in their special enclosures until the ground has been cleared of everybody else, I at least consider remaining there myself, as a gesture of solidarity until they are free to go. But somehow an extra drink with the directors in the boardroom never quite seems like a sacrifice. So I complain to the senior police officer who is sharing the club's hospitality, marvel at the good temper of the men and women who are kept fastened in pens like wayward cattle, and leave when I think the traffic has cleared.

Sometimes I cross paths with Sheffield Wednesday supporters being escorted to their trains. It often looks like an extract from the Colditz story. At Southampton, three mounted policemen preceded what seemed to be an armoured car. They were followed by a footpatrol. The whole column was completed by a second reinforced vehicle and another half dozen mounted officers. In between the guardians of the law were approximately fifty Wednesday supporters, anxious to make their sad way home. Fortunately, despite their treatment they remained convinced that they were law-abiding citizens who wanted to do nothing better than travel in peace.

When in the days of football's postwar soccer glory I stood on the Spion Kop, I would have found it almost impossible to believe any prophet who told me that, by the time I reached middle age, the football supporter would have become regarded as a menace to society. Of course, menace a few of them are. I have been tyrannized in the stand at Chelsea and I have been terrified at Millwall. But it is not simply sentiment that convinces me that the overwhelming majority of football supporters are the same sort of men and women as those with whom I spent long Saturdays. Then, everybody who paid one and sixpence went to watch football. Now, a tiny proportion go looking for trouble. The duty of police and government is to separate one from the other. There will be no solution to football violence if the vast majority of law-abiding fans are treated like hooligans with flick knives in their pockets and razor blades sewn into the peaks of their caps. I learned that forty years ago on the Spion Kop.

Of course football has changed. But it has changed with society. In the bad old days directors believed that they owned players. When Danny Blanchflower was sold to Aston Villa, the chairman of Barnsley did the deal over lunch in the Sheffield Grand Hotel. The best wing half in England had a sandwich with the chairman's chauffeur in the waiter's kitchen. In that era of slavery and servitude players were paid a pittance for providing a fortune in entertainment. Don Revie told me that when he played at Wembley he was promised a £2 bonus if he won and £1 for the draw. The desirable changes which have made football a less feudal institution have brought with them all sorts of penalties. And the violence which now lurks in every corner of our society, like the avarice which is encouraged from the highest places, has done the game enormous damage. But the principle has not changed since those days at Hillsborough – days when my father prophesied that the record transfer fee of £30,000 which Sheffield Wednesday paid for Eddie Quigley would ruin the game for ever.

Football does more than provide unrivalled pleasure on a Saturday afternoon. It keeps us in romantic association with our individual and collective past. It is a game of industrial England, generally played in crowded cities. It is no longer the exclusive preserve of men and women who work in the mines and factories. For the mines and factories are not the force they used to be in England's economy. But in general, it is the game of the sons and daughters of that old working class.

The new supporters want and deserve improved amenities. They are not satisfied to stand all afternoon on shale terraces and then gratefully shake the grit out of their shoes before they walk home. They want cafeterias and car parks, family enclosures and roofs to protect them from the rain. They even want lavatories they can visit without risk to their lives and health. And some of them – though not all – want a seat at a price they can afford for themselves and their families. But they are still part of that old spirit of competitive loyalty, identification with a town and a team and the history of achievement that goes back almost 100 years.

That is not a feeling which is always shared by the salesmen in the executive boxes or even by the directors who have arrived recently on the football scene because they know that owning a club brings them social cudos, civic respect and political influence. But it is the feeling of the men who have spent their Saturday afternoons on the uncovered terraces. Anyone who does not feel an irrational loyalty towards a football club is missing an important part of life. Anyone who feels it to such a degree that on each Saturday afternoon he is overtaken with the fear that he will not get into the ground, enjoys the special privilege and special pleasure of being a real supporter.

When I look back on all the things that happened to me in the 1950s – the pressure to pass examinations, the persuasion to part my hair, the prohibition of crepe-soled shoes – I recall with affection the one great advantage that I enjoyed at that time. I was taught how to be a proper football supporter.

Willis Hall

Willis has seen and played in more than a few games of football, but the one for Gerry's XI against Ford Open Prison remains most firmly in his mind. A Yorkshireman, he has been writing for the theatre, television and cinema for over thirty years. His latest book, The Vampire's Holiday, *will be published, by Collins, in 1991.*

An Open Game

WILLIS HALL

We have a wonderful harmonium in the dressing room.

Ivor Powell, ex-Bradford City manager

'I remember, I remember . . .'

To be absolutely honest though, for the most part I tend to forget. And dragging from soccer's yesteryear my most memorable match is, for this particular football fan, a daunting task. The soccer section of my mind is a ragbag of games, goals and half-remembered footballing ghosts. And I don't think I would want it any other way. I half admire but half deplore those soccer enthusiasts who can trot out, parrot fashion, entire teams from the mists of time. Personally speaking, I have reached an age when I can reasonably claim forgetfulness.

These days my most favourite match ever was the last one I attended – my most exciting match, the very next one I shall get to. Already this year, for instance, I have not only played as a striker for Halifax Town, I have also been instrumental in their gaining promotion and winning the League Cup. Well, admittedly it was only on my youngest son's Footballer of the Year computer game, but when you get to my age (and I speak as the proud possessor of a senior citizen's rail card), it is achievements such as these that stand out in the memory.

Was it, I often wonder, fickleness or sheer perversity on my father's part when, in a burst of Leeds United idolatry, he had christened me with the name of his favourite Leeds United player of the 1930s, Willis Edwards, and then, within a season, switched his own affections to Hunslet Rugby League Club?

Whatever the reason, I have inherited my old man's butterfly-like inconsistency, flitting in my allegiances from one club to the next. The soccer side of my life has been both pleasurable to the fan in me and fruitful to the writer, down all the years – starting as a supporter on the terraces at Elland Road and, later, at Craven Cottage (during Johnny Haynes's golden days), progressing to president at St Albans City FC in the Isthmian League times (while doubling as a patron of a Sunday morning set up), whence to a seat in Brentford's boardroom in the 1970s.

And now the footballing wheel has turned full circle and I am back into watching from the terraces in my native north of England and at any ground that takes my fancy, in company with the youngest son who is acquiring, as Saturday follows close on Saturday, a boy's enthusiasm for the game that it is a sheer joy to share. Although it deserves to be mentioned too, in passing, that I am a supporter of Sliema Wanderers, a club in Malta where I have a second home.

And out of all these years, and all my teams, and all their games, and with a failing memory, I have to plump for one single, solitary fixture that stands head and shoulders above all the others.

Impossible, you ask?

Well, no. As a matter of fact, there is one particular football match that always comes immediately to mind, whenever I sit down on any out-of-season Saturday afternoon and, for want of something better to do, browse through the fading pages of the soccer scrapbook inside my head. I ought to admit though, before I begin to regale you with an account of those particular 90 minutes, that I cannot remember the final score. I do remember the names of some of the players – well, on our side, at least, for I was one of them myself. But, rack my brains as I may, I will not be able to tell you whether we won or lost. I only know that it was the finest afternoon of soccer in my entire life. Neither could I tell you the year in which this magical match took place – the closest I can come to pinning it down is to say that it was during those heady footballing times of the mid-to-late 1960s, when the intoxicating afterglow of England's World Cup triumph still hung across the country; and when I myself was still young enough, and fit enough, to pull on and lace up a pair of soccer boots without gasping for breath unduly.

What I do remember though, and clearly, are the events that led up to that afternoon of rare enjoyment. They began with a telephone call:

'Is that Willis Hall?' asked the voice on the other end of the line.

'It is.'

My caller identified himself. He was an actor I had worked with and whose features would be instantly recognizable to the regular TV viewer.

'Is it true,' he continued, 'that you're connected with a Sunday celebrity soccer side which turns out for charity and that sort of malarky?'

'Well, yes' – but it was only partly true. I was involved with a Sunday side which boasted a couple of showbiz players on its books and which had been known to fit in the occasional charity fixture. But, when the chips were down, we much preferred the anonymity of playing against north London pub teams. It was not that we were opposed to supporting worthy causes – but we enjoyed the free-and-easy pint-and-a-pie camaraderie of the ale house far more than the marquee-housed genteel finger buffet respectability that went hand in hand with charity football. Besides, I have long held the belief that playing football for football's sake is one of the worthiest causes on God's earth.

In addition to the showbiz celebs, we numbered several ex-league footballers on our books. A quartet of old Fulham players (Johnny Haynes, Jimmy Hill, Bill Dodgin and Tom Wilson) turned out regularly, Dave Sexton, then manager at Chelsea, played his share of games, and (whisper it gently) a couple of pro players still in the game would enjoy a clandestine match with us, unbeknown to their managers. Also included occasionally on the teamsheet were a couple of National Hunt jockeys; a pro boxer; two bookmakers and, infrequently, a Marseilles restaurateur – a brick-built karsey of a man who made a formidable fullback.

In short we were a catholic bunch of chaps united by a common love of soccer. Our captain, mentor and enthusiastic organizer was an ex-Fulham and ex-Watford goalkeeper, the late Dave Underwood, a kindly, rugged but gentle man. When we had formed the team on a drunken spree Dave came up with a suggestion for a teamstrip that pleased everyone.

''Ang about!' he had said, his cockney voice breaking in on the fierce debate ranging across the pub table. 'We'll play in Argentina's colours.'

'Why Argentina?' asked several puzzled founder members.

'Listen to this,' he advised them. 'Blue and white vertical stripes, black shorts . . .' he paused, keeping us all on tenterhooks, and then added: '. . . and dove-grey stockings.' The dove-grey stockings won us over.

We called ourselves Gerry's XI after a Soho theatrical drinking club, and in the faint hope that the establishment would grant honorary membership to all our players. That did not come to pass, but Gerry's Club, at least, did grant us the right to pin our fixtures and teamsheets on its noticeboard.

And thus, to come full circle, had the actor who telephoned me come to learn of our existence.

'What can I do for you?' I asked him. 'Are you looking for a game?'

'Well, sort of . . .'

He was playing it very cagey but, eventually, he explained his problem. He had a brother who was doing time in Ford Open Prison. The brother was allowed two visits a month (I think), but had a long list of both friends and relatives anxious to see him. Because of his brother's busy social visiting calendar, the actor's turn at the visiting pass did not come round all that regularly. It had reached the actor's ears that Gerry's XI played the Ford Open Nick XI, on occasion. The actor's brother was a regular in the prison team. If we could arrange a run out in our team, a brotherly reunion would be effected, over and above prison visiting regulations.

It was, it seemed to me, a reasonable enough request. Also it was true that Gerry's XI had made the odd journey down to the south coast and played friendlies against the prison team. They were among our most enjoyable fixtures. Ford Open Nick were a hospitable lot. Their team was made up of both screws and cons. They were fitter than us by far – they had a couple of physical training instructors playing up front, both of them dead keen fitness fanatics. But we considered ourselves a more skilful side and, anyway, could look to our Marseilles restaurateur to contain the pair of PTI strikers.

I told my actor caller that I could not promise anything, but that I would see what could be done. As it happened, things turned out quite nicely for all concerned. The prison team had got themselves into the semi-finals of some competition and were delighted at the prospect of a warm-up friendly – particularly against Gerry's XI with its goodly sprinkling of ex-pro players who would provide worthwhile opposition without aggro. (We didn't tell them we might be playing the Marseilles fullback.)

The fixture fitted nicely in with our plans too. A coach trip to the seaside was always welcome. The post-match hospitality at Ford, though simple fare (meat-paste sandwiches, biscuits, prison fruit cake, metal jugs of tea), was abundant. And although pints of beer were not forthcoming inside the wire mesh fence, there were ample welcoming hostelries on the road back to London. Plus the fact that we had a new player who was in need of a run out before being thrust into the hurly burly of Sunday morning north London pub soccer.

The author and playwright, Bill Naughton, a chum of mine, had put in his formal request to join our ranks. At that time, Bill was playing regularly in Hyde Park in the makeshift spontaneous soccer matches that took place on most weekday afternoons. The teams were mostly made up of Italian and Spanish waiters taking a break between luncheon and dinner duties. Soccer boots were obligatory but, those apart, it was a case of play as you are. The occasional soup-spotted dinner jacket was to be observed doing duty as a goalpost. Bill was wont to take his boots along, knotted around his neck, and hang about on a touchline looking hungry for football.

It was enthusiasm such as that for which Gerry's XI was always on the lookout. Our only slight concern was that Bill Naughton was several years on the wrong side of fifty and it was wondered whether he had the stamina for a full 90 minutes of football. The Ford Open Nick fixture would provide us with the opportunity to put that to the test.

Thus it was then, that our team coach set out from central London for the south coast early-ish one late summer morning in the 1960s. A pre-match light lunch had been booked in Brighton: fillet steak and toast – the footballer's food of that day. It was back in the good old times, remember, before the dieticians took over with their pre-match dishes of boiled chicken. It is rarely referred to these days, but England won the World Cup on fillet steaks and toast.

After lunch, with the half-digested steaks sitting comfortably inside our stomachs, we reboarded the coach and set out on the final leg of the journey. Our guest actor, around whom this story is loosely spun, had declined our offer of lunch in Brighton and had suggested instead that we pick him up several miles outside the prison.

As the coach trundled along a lonely coastal road, we suddenly saw him up ahead, a solitary figure leaning, in an actorish sort of way, on a fence close by a fringe of trees. He waved at us, cheerfully, as the coach drew up and then instead of clambering on board, turned and gestured towards the trees. To our surprise, a dozen or so ladies stepped out of the woodland and crossed towards where the coach was parked. They all carried bulging carrier bags in both hands. It was an entirely unexpected happening and I got down from the coach to challenge the actor as to their identities. They were, he told me, girlfriends or wives of prison inmates. The actor's brother, it seemed, was not the only convict in need of an unscheduled visit.

'I thought that we could smuggle them into the nick as our team's wives and girlfriends,' the actor explained, diffidently. I looked across at the knot of ladies and they returned my dubious glance with cheery smiles.

'What are in the carrier bags?' I asked the actor.

'Oh, just a few nibbles. For a bit of a snack after the game.'

He had spoken with a fine, professional sense of understatement. The carrier bags, it turned out, were bulging with all manner of good things: a half dozen cold roast chickens; bowls of potato salad; fresh crusty rolls thick with butter; lots of lettuce; tomatoes – food sufficient for a feast.

'Are you allowed to take all that food into the prison?' I asked him, unsurely.

The actor shrugged. 'Not exactly,' he told me. 'But I thought that we might smuggle that in as well – at the bottom of the team hamper, underneath the strip.'

It was at this point I noticed that he, too, was carrying a carrier bag. The contents clinked ominously.

'What have you got in there?' I said.

'Just these,' he told me, lifting out two litre-sized wine bottles, both of which contained a yellowish liquid.

'Isn't that going just a titch too far,' I asked him, 'taking booze into the nick?'

'Oh, it isn't drink,' he explained. 'It's vinaigrette dressing.'

'Vinaigrette dressing?'

'Every Sunday afternoon, the cons get salad for tea. With the salad they get salad cream. My brother can't stand salad cream. Mum's made him up two bottles of his favourite vinaigrette dressing. There's enough here to keep him going until he gets out.'

Correct me if you know better, but it's my belief that Gerry's XI are the only football team to have smuggled two litres of vinaigrette dressing into one of Her Majesty's prisons. We got the rest in through the gates too, without any difficulty at all: prisoners' wives and girlfriends, roast chickens, all the trimmings.

We changed, with the opposing team, in the prison gymnasium. I seem to remember that they played in Manchester United's colours. They cast many an envious glance at our Argentinian strip – particularly the dove-grey stockings. As we trotted out onto the pitch, a ragged cheer went up from the touchlines which were deep with cons. Bill Naughton, who was running alongside me, suddenly snatched at a sharp intake of breath.

'What's up, Bill?' I asked him, with some concern, wondering if, perhaps, the sprint from the changing room to the pitch had been too much for the over fifty-year-old? Nothing of the kind.

'Look!' he replied, pointing down at one of the goalmouths and with wonder in his voice. 'The goal posts have got nets!'

He went on to tell me that although he had played football all his life, from his schoolboy days in Lancashire to his Hyde Park continental waiters' encounters, he had only rarely played with real goal posts and he had never ever played with goal posts that had nets. He was about to fulfil a lifetime's ambition.

I don't know whether it was the goal nets or the dove-grey stockings that motivated Bill that afternoon, but he played out of his skin. He roved along the right wing for all of the 90 minutes, an inspired grey-haired dynamo of a man in his mid-fifties. The spectators took him to their hearts. 'Naughton! Naughton!' went up from the makeshift terraces.

Oh, but I enjoyed that afternoon. And if the game was good the post-match shindig was magic. It took place in the prison gymnasium and was attended by all the players, the match officials, and the ladies who had infiltrated onto our coach. There were groaning tables laden with cold roast chicken, potato salad, lettuce, tomatoes, meat-paste sandwiches, biscuits, prison fruit cake and huge metal jugs brimming with steaming tea. It deserves to be stated, too, that the vinaigrette dressing was out of this world.

As I said at the beginning, I can't remember whether our side won or lost. The most important thing about that fixture was that the result was entirely unimportant. It was an afternoon of rare soccer enjoyment – and only soccer provides such afternoons. I rang Jimmy Hill the other day to ask him if he remembered the result.

'You played in that Gerry's XI game at Ford,' I put to him, 'when we smuggled in the women and the grub.'

There was a short pause at the other end before he spoke. 'No, Willis, I missed out on that one. I've often heard about it though. Haynsey played and Bill Dodgin and Tom Wilson. It is still talked about. I wish I had been there.'

Well, I was there, and it will be with me always. Oddly enough, Bill Naughton never played for Gerry's XI again. I think that the goal nets coupled with the dove-grey stockings had provided him with the ultimate soccer experience and to have attempted to repeat it would have been gilding the lily.

Several years afterwards, I was strolling through Hyde Park, mulling over a plot line as we dramatists are inclined to do. The Spanish and Italian waiters were there, as always, in profusion and knocking balls about all over the place. I looked out for a grey-haired, ageing dynamo, but he was not there that afternoon. I did bump into another acquaintance though – a tracksuited figure jogging round the perimeters of the makeshift pitches. It was Don Revie. I had interviewed him a couple of times and, with my Leeds connections, knew him well enough to swap pleasantries. Those were the days when Revie was the England manager. The Football Association's headquarters at Lancaster Gate were but a long throw-in away from Hyde Park. Unlike Bill Naughton though, Don Revie did not take himself off into the park in search of a kick-about with the continental waiters. He was only concerned with his personal fitness.

When I heard about Revie's daily Hyde Park solitary training stints, they seemed to provide a curiously unsatisfactory lifestyle for a man who, in his Leeds United days, had counted so much on the family spirit. He had created, at Elland Road, arguably the finest football family in the game. He had always been a tracksuit manager who had thoroughly enjoyed taking training and revelled in the close proximity of his players. As England manager, he now found himself attempting to engender a family spirit into a squad of players who would get together eight times a year at the very most.

Separated also from his own close-knit family and living in a characterless London hotel room, Don Revie was spending his afternoons running around the perimeters of football pitches populated by continental waiters.

'Aren't you finding it rather lonely?' I asked him. And, having put the question, it immediately occurred to me that 'lonely' was a foolish adjective to attach to the man who was at the very hub of England's football. 'Perhaps "lonely" isn't quite the right word,' I added, hastily.

'Lonely?' he echoed, paused – and in his rich flow of words, Don Revie did not pause often – then: 'Lonely is the right word,' he said, without a trace of sadness but with a great deal of meaning.

South of Sheffield, Don Revie is remembered mostly as the man who turned his back on England. Up here in the north, he is revered as the man who created the best Leeds United side that ever was.

Soccer, of course, is all things to all men. At the lower end of the pecking order it can mean delighting in the camaraderie of post-match meat-paste sandwiches and tomato salad with vinaigrette dressing, with Gerry's XI and the home team at Ford Open Nick. Conversely, at the very top of the pile, it can mean being condemned to a lonely lifestyle: a solitary, tracksuited figure, a long way from home, jogging around a score of makeshift pitches where waiters' dinner jackets serve as goal posts.

Eric Dunning

Eric is a Professor of Sociology at Leicester University, but is probably equally proud of his five years at centre half for the University as a graduate and post-graduate, 1957–61, or even his earlier performances for Hayes A-team. After a spell studying in St Louis, he settled to teach at Leicester. Along with John Williams and Patrick Murphy, he runs the Norman Chester Research Centre, from where they have written three studies of football hooliganism.

On Being and Becoming a Leicester City Fan

ERIC DUNNING

I'm a connoisseur of failure. I can smell it, roll it round my mouth,
tell you the vintage and the side of the hill that grew it.

Giles Cooper, 'Unman, Wittering and Zigo', radio drama

I have deliberately given this piece a longish and rather obscure title.
For an existentialist philosopher, of course, the first four words would
probably have been enough. But then it's difficult to imagine an
existentialist or any other kind of philosopher – with the obvious
exception of that famous Spurs fan, the late Freddie Ayer – stooping
so low as to discuss anything so trivial as support for a football team.
I'm a sociologist however, and proud of it. I'm also proud of being a
Leicester City supporter.

Sociology is a discipline with firm traditions of logical and empirical
study, which is more than can be said for supporting Leicester City; I
am none too certain of the rational basis for this. You have to be some
kind of nut to support such a 'nearly' team, a side which frequently
promises much but delivers little: four FA Cup appearances since the
war and the losers each time, yo-yoing between the First and Second
Divisions and occasionally threatening to go even lower but so far
thankfully avoiding the ranks of the Football League's associate members.

Can my support for such a nearly team be rationally explained?
Although I have lived in Leicester for more than thirty years, I am not
a native. If I can be forgiven for using just one piece of sociological
jargon, my status as a City fan was 'achieved' rather than 'ascribed'. I
was born in 1936 in Hayes, about two miles from Heathrow Airport.
Deep down, I still think of myself principally as a Londoner.

My parents, especially my father, were sports orientated and very
keen on sport for boys. According to family legend, my maternal

163

grandfather was one of the combatants in the last bare-fisted prizefight to take place on Chiswick's Turnham Green. When he was in the army in the 1920s, my father had the occasional professional fight. His greatest claim to sporting fame was that he once fought an exhibition bout against 'Bombardier' Billy Wells. My father hailed from Norfolk and remained a keen Norwich City fan until his death in 1981. He would, I'm sure, have loved to see their present team. After leaving the army, he became a London bus driver and one of his conductors in the 1940s had played for Queen's Park Rangers. His name was Jack Chapman and I have a clear memory of Jack demonstrating his ball skills to me in our garden. I must have been nine or ten at the time. Jack was nearer fifty, but probably as sharp as many I have played football with since.

Neither Jack Chapman nor my father gave me my first serious lessons in the arts of football. That honour fell to my elder brother, Roy. He was a wing half and it was while watching him play for Hayes A-team in the early 1950s that I saw a footballing genius who later came to manage Leicester City's greatest postwar side. I was thirteen or fourteen, and playing for the A-side on that cold, wet November day was a sixteen-year-old inside forward called Jimmy Bloomfield. Of course, neither he nor I had the faintest inkling that our futures were destined to take us both to Leicester. Nor did I realize that I, too, would later play for the Hayes A-team, a fact which enables me to boast feebly that I played for the same team as Jimmy Bloomfield. (I don't mention the fact that my few games for them were six years later.)

It was not the attractive Bloomfield side of the 1970s that led me to follow what has now become my favourite football team. I came to Leicester in 1956 and was too involved in playing football for the university to watch much professional football. I did occasionally see the 1956–7 team though which, with players like Jack Froggatt, Johnny Morris and Arthur Rowley, won promotion to the First Division. Rowley, I remember, was nicknamed the 'Pudding' by the crowd on account of his bulk. He nevertheless managed to score forty-four goals that season.

It was in 1968, while French students ran wild in Paris, that I began to go wild about Leicester City, and my playing days came to an end. A younger colleague, Ivan Waddington, had before coming to the university played a few games for Leyton Orient reserves. The ease with which he left me for dead in a staff match was central in making me realize that the time had come to retire. Two or three seasons earlier and I'd have either got the ball or he'd have ended up flat on his back.

Around the same time I went to Filbert Street with Ivan to watch Leicester City's Fourth Round FA Cup replay against Manchester City. They had drawn 0–0 at Maine Road and in the replay the Foxes quickly went 2–0 down. However, they turned the tables in an exciting second half with goals from Rodney Fern, Frank Large (2) and David Nish, eventually emerging as 4–3 winners. I vividly remember that at that game I really cared for the first time about who won. That was it. Since 1969 I have watched the majority of Leicester's home matches and quite a few away from home as well. Since 1980 I have taken my son Michael, a born and bred, and 'ascribed' supporter, who is now fourteen.

Fate chose a year of mixed fortunes for me in which to transfer my footballing interests from the field to the terraces. It may not be widely remembered outside football circles in the city but in 1968–9 Leicester City achieved a remarkable double, losing an FA Cup Final and being relegated to the Second Division. I went to Wembley and saw them lose to a vastly superior Manchester City, who should have won by considerably more than 1–0. The Foxes were no match for a team containing the likes of Colin Bell, Francis Lee and Mike Summerbee. There had been, however, some compensations. One was savouring the delight of beating Liverpool 1–0 in a Fifth-Round replay at Anfield. (It is one of Leicester City fans' few joys to have achieved the feat of beating Liverpool so often over the years that they have become rather one of their bogey teams.) The other compensation was a young goalkeeper called Peter Shilton. To put it mildly, he quickly proved a more than adequate replacement for Gordon Banks, a player whom many City fans had believed to be irreplaceable when he was transferred to Stoke in 1967.

In 1970–1, however, after only two seasons in the Second Division, Leicester City were back in the big time, managed by Frank O'Farrell. A little known thing regarding their successful promotion campaign is the fact that the total of fourteen goals officially recorded as having been conceded by Peter Shilton – it was the season in which he won his first full England cap – is actually one short. Shilton was beaten by a powerful header in the match against Portsmouth but the ball hit a stanchion and rebounded into play with the referee unaware that a goal had been scored. Those of us at the Leicester end could see it clearly, though, and were both amazed and relieved at such a rare refereeing blunder.

Immediately after helping the Foxes to secure their restoration to a higher level, O'Farrell was snatched away by Manchester United, only quickly to fall victim to the club's voracious demand for immediate continuation of the Matt Busby glory days. The Irishman's loss, however, turned out to be Leicester's gain. He was replaced by Jimmy Bloomfield, manager of Leyton Orient since his playing days had ended in 1969. Jimmy didn't know it but a terrace regular throughout his tenure at Filbert Street was another west Londoner, one who'd also played for the A-team at Hayes.

To this day, Leicester City fans still argue fiercely over which of the club's postwar sides has been their finest. For me, though and, I suspect, for most people who watched the Foxes between 1971 and 1977, it's a matter beyond dispute. Earlier City sides may have reached the FA Cup Final on four occasions. The Matt Gillies side may actually have won the League Cup in 1963-4. By contrast the best achieved under Bloomfield was to reach the semi-finals of the FA Cup in 1973-4 (drawing 0–0 with Liverpool only to be beaten 3–1 in the replay at Villa Park), and to have finished seventh in the First Division in 1975-6. Nevertheless the 'nearly' side which Bloomfield put together outranks the others. The superlative Shilton, ably backed by defenders Graham Cross ('the tank'), Dennis Rofe and Steve Whitworth, gave them a solidity at the back on which the midfield and the attack were able to build. In midfield, they had the under-rated Jon Sammels, bought from Arsenal for £100,000 after a hate campaign from the Highbury crowd, and with whom Bloomfield experimented unsuccessfully in a Beckenbauer-type *libero* role, the ill-fated 'S-plan'. Then there was Alan Birchenall, still at the club as public relations officer. No mean player and always likely to amuse the crowd with his bubbling sense of fun and sometimes to thrill them with shots from his powerful left foot. But it was up front with the artistry of Keith Weller and Frank Worthington that the Bloomfield side really excelled. Comparisons are difficult but for me Weller was usually the more effective, skilful and exciting of the two. I shall always remember his hat trick against Liverpool in 1972. City had gone 2–0 down to goals by John Toshack, and Weller's performance, particularly in the second half, was nothing short of stunning. It is, I think, put into perspective by the fact that it was not until 1983 that another player – Terry Gibson of Coventry – scored three goals in one match against the Reds.

I could list many other memorable matches and goals scored by the Bloomfield team. I think, though, that what he and the team achieved is best summed up by an extract from a report which appeared in the *Sunday Times*, in February 1974, following their 4–0 victory over Luton Town in the FA Cup:

> If you savour football as a pure game of entertainment, character and, of course, spectacular goals, you should share with me the hope that Leicester City reach Wembley next May. They simply ran amok at Luton with all the culture, imagination and ball skills we have long believed to be either things of the past or secrets guarded by men of darker skins from far-off Brazil.
>
> Leicester's first goal after 18 minutes was of such quality and entertainment that if they do, as their manager predicted long ago, reach Wembley they can lift the status of football, even of the nation. It was that good: class and enterprise, understanding and confidence which raises the game to that of art form.

The scorers that day were Weller, Worthington and Steve Earle (2). Unfortunately, though, Bloomfield's Leicester City remained a nearly team, like the others. It failed to reach Wembley or win any of the honours they were capable of achieving. Why they came so close but ultimately failed is difficult to say. Perhaps it had something to do with directors incapable of matching the flair of Bloomfield and his players with boardroom nous. Suffice to say that, although Leicester finished a respectable eleventh in the First Division in 1976–7, this constituted failure relative to the expectations that had been gener-ated by Bloomfield and his side. A voluble 'Bloomfield out' campaign developed among sections of the crowd and he resigned. I have always suspected that it may not have been an entirely voluntary decision and that the pressure Bloomfield suffered may have had something to do with his tragically early death in 1983. One thing, though, is certain: Jimmy Bloomfield was not the kind of man who would have gloated when his successor, Frank McLintock, disastrously guided City to relegation in his first and only season.

Subsequent Leicester City sides have again flattered to deceive more often than not. Under Jock Wallace and Gordon Milne – ably assisted on the field by the likes of Gary Lineker, Alan Smith, Russell Osman and Ian Wilson, they did chalk up one or two notable successes. All too often though, star players, the most recent being Mike Newell, have been sold to make ends meet. In any case the club was unable during the 1980s to satisfy the reasonable desire of such players to play at the highest level with all that that means in terms of finance, intrinsic satisfaction and prestige.

Of all the Leicester teams since 1977, the present one under David Pleat has come closest to recapturing the magic of the Bloomfield days. They haven't yet managed this consistently but when they are on song they are a delight to watch. I don't think the similarities between Pleat and Bloomfield are accidental. Pleat, too, is one of football's thinkers. And he is capable of managing on a shoestring. Above all, he is deeply committed to the view that winning is best achieved with style, artistry and flair. It is a mark of Pleat's strength of character – and also, it has to be added, of the vision of the Leicester City board – that at Leicester he has managed to resurrect his career following the vilification he suffered at the hands of the tabloid press during his days as manager of Spurs.

His strength of character makes me suspect – though of course I have no logical basis for saying so – that this will be the last of the nearly teams.

Will Buckley

Will first watched Chelsea when they lost to Everton 2–1 in the 1970–1 FA Charity Shield. Since then he has followed them through all their ups and downs. After an education which taught him 'only to walk past great architecture without noticing it' he embarked on a legal career. Having held down a wide range of jobs, from photo-copying to asking for adjournments, he is now a freelance lawyer, who sits at home; while waiting for fusion he writes for various magazines.

Odds and Sods

WILL BUCKLEY

All life is 6–5 against.

Damon Runyan

The bookmakers were offering Woking at 2–1. So on Saturday 18 November 1989 I found myself setting off for Wexham Park, home of Slough Town, rather than Stamford Bridge. To be honest it was some-thing of a relief to be avoiding the Bridge for, check your Rothmans if you must, Chelsea were sitting on top of the league. You might think that someone who had supported Chelsea for nearly two decades and who had witnessed the outstanding moment of that period when Colin Pates lifted the Full Members Cup, would have left Saint and Greavsie early to get to the Shed in good time. Not a bit of it. I was bewildered and frightened by Chelsea's inexplicable surge. The improbable had finally occurred and the inevitable come-down would be painful. I knew the rest of the season would be akin to watching an ex-girlfriend perform ineptly with a new lover: I would be overcome by irritation with the team selection and depression at the same old errors being trotted out. I would become increasingly unhappy. Much better to be at Wexham Park for the First Round FA Cup tie between Slough Town and Woking. Better off not only emotionally but finan-cially for the bookies had not done their homework.

Woking at 2–1. At first glance, bearing in mind that Woking were in the Vauxhall-Opel League First Division and Slough were in the Pre-mier and at home, this quote might not appear over generous. But those in the know could see it was a snip. Woking were on a roll hav-ing trounced Lewes 6–0 and enjoyed an emphatic 5–1 victory at Kingstonian. They were unbeaten, scoring at will and favourites for the Surrey Demolition Senior Cup. The crucial form line was pro-vided by Boreham Wood. Woking had dispatched them 4–0 yet Boreham Wood had defeated Slough. What is more, earlier in the week Slough had tumbled out of the AC Delco Cup. It was a treble star, sell your hi-fi, beautiful bloody certainty.

A certainty, moreover, which you could bet on. Bookmakers are notoriously cagey if they so much as sniff a fix and they remain wary about football betting. On a normal league Saturday the punter has to bet in quintuples if he includes a home result, or trebles if he concentrates on the draws and aways. Now, as everyone knows, multiple betting is a spectacularly quick way to lose your wad. By the end of the afternoon you are reduced to a plethora of 'ifs'. If Chelsea had won, if United had drawn, and if City had pulled one back. . . . However, on Cup matches a single win bet is allowed.

Not only was there in this case a giveaway price but very few people appeared to be in the know. As far as I could tell only Mickey, Neighbour – strangely enough the bloke who lived next door to him – and Sean the Spread had the necessary information. Mickey had spotted the bookmakers' gaffe. An optimistic if catastrophic punter, he would often leave the track early in order to catch Woking at Erith and Belvedere, Leyton Wingate or the Met. Police. Short yet unambitious, he had dedicated years of his life to dodging and weaving around the racecourses of Britain in the pursuit of value. It could not be denied that he had a 52 per cent winning rate in the Cambridgeshire, but he had never learned not to bet on other races.

At last it appeared his hours of research would bring a pay off. He had told Neighbour by mistake, and Sean the Spread had in turn let me in as he had fond memories of the little fortune we had made offering pessimistic students most ungenerous odds on their finals results. 'If you do better than expected you'll be happy. If not, you'll be able to afford a couple of bottles of vodka' was the easy patter. I had reinvested the proceeds on a doubting social anthropologist, while Sean had purchased a suit as good as the Next man's and got a job in the City. Now, three years on, he is dealing bonds with finesse and is responsible for some of the tightest spreads in the Square Mile. In his office he has three TV screens (regular with dish, SEAQ and Scandinavian), three phones (internal, external and dicta) and three sofas. In his flat he has Kathy de Klerk who trades diamonds for De Beers and models them for Sunday magazines. He is driven by ambition, greed and a chauffeur called Tom. I, meanwhile, had my telephone confiscated at work, have a truculent fridge in my Hither Green bedsit and do not possess a driving licence. Nonetheless, although I could no longer afford to bet against him, it was good to be betting with him.

For a time, early in my gambling career, I had done my money on the owner's butcher's tip or the trainer's publican's selection before realizing that if this information was reaching my ears it was clearly duff. This time would be different; the expertise was sound and the exposure limited. As, I think, management consultants say, you are only as good as the information at your disposal. We were very good.

Saturday morning, early, I visited William Hill's. 'Excuse me, this 2–1 against Woking on your coupon here. Is that the price you're still offering?'

'Yes, if that's what it says on the coupon, that's what we're offering.'

'And if the team are 2–1 against I can use this table on the back to discover the correct score odds?' I asked.

'Yes chum. I think you'll find that the coupon is self-explanatory. We do take some care in compiling them.'

'OK. I'll have a ton on Woking to win at 2–1 plus the tax, and a pony each on Woking 3–0 at 33s, Woking 3–1 at 25s, Woking 4–0 at 100s, and Woking 4–1 at 100s, with the tax on each.'

'You what?'

'Don't worry I'll write it down for you. Here's £220.'

Now before any professional starts giving me stick for betting on the correct scores – normally a mug's bet to be sure – you should realize that I required a big win, for my legal career, which had never been promising, was now in tatters. The profession which had provided me with the funds for a moderate assault on the bookmakers had run dry. A few days earlier, a woman partner in the firm, and in the club, had called me in.

'Hi, how's the baby? Scan go OK?' I crawled.

'Will, I called you in to discuss *your* future not my child's. Frankly you've got to decide whether you want to be a lawyer.'

'Er . . .'

'If you decide that you do want to be a lawyer I have to advise you that your future is bleak.'

'What's my future like if I decide that I don't want to be a lawyer?'

'Exactly.'

I reeled out of that conversation only to find the company hitman sitting in my chair. A doubly unfortunate bloke this one, being both bald and bearded.

'Will, are you still here?'

'Yes.'

'You want my opinion of you as a lawyer? In all honesty and speaking from the shoulder I'd have to rate you, on a scale of one to a hundred, damn near one.'

I thought about pleading for an extra decimal place but realized it would be futile and went and sat on the toilet for the rest of the afternoon. Reappearing from the closet I discovered on my desk a copy of the *Law Society Gazette* left open at the jobs page. Strangely there was a very small advertisement announcing that my position was vacant. The job was lost, but there was always Woking.

Mickey, Neighbour and Sean the Spread were already ensconced in the car park of a pub near the ground.

'Welcome, Will. What did you get on at?' asked Mickey.

'I took the twos on offer at William Hill's.'

'There you go. Yet again, I've got the value. Surrey Racing were offering 9-4 between ten and eleven on Wednesday morning,' said Sean the Spread.

'Yeah I know all that but that was before Slough got dumped out of the AC Delco Cup. That must have upset them.'

'I knew I should have backed them to win 5-0,' quipped Sean the Spread.

Neighbour looked pensive. 'Take me through that Boreham Wood form line again Mickey.'

'Neighbour, no worries. It's all written down here. Cast your eye over it, take in the Bognor result, see what they did to the Corinthian Casuals. It's a doddle, a licence to print money.'

'Mickey, I know all the form, but who's actually playing for Woking?'

'Well, the lads to look out for are Colin Caulfield between the sticks who once had a spell at Wimbledon. Big hands. Then there's Trevor Baron at the back who's a sort of Vauxhall First Division South Des Walker. Running things in midfield is Mark Biggins who we bought from Windsor and Eton for £2000.'

'Two grand?' exclaimed Sean the Spread.

'Yeah, a club record,' replied Mickey.

'Christ, I could buy this club,' concluded Sean.

'When we win pal, when we win. Anyhow, to continue, up front we've got Paul "Scouse" Mulvaney and Tim Buzaglo. Scouse is only a little lad but he can rise like a block of flats if the occasion demands it and Buzaglo . . . Buzaglo . . . He's a joy.' Silence descended on the group as we all considered this final statement. It was broken by an increasingly twitchy Neighbour.

'Come on boys, kick-off's in half an hour. We want to get a decent position.'

Neighbour is one of those dreadful punters who insists on tempering your natural enthusiasm with entirely rational worrying. Even worse he's constantly reminding you of a Charlie Smirke treble he got up in the mid-1950s, which was possibly his last win. Certainly I've never seen anyone lose money so grudgingly, so consistently and in such small sums as Neighbour. He was more nervous than ever on that day. He was probably in too deep, but then none of us were going to look that clever if Woking blew it.

Non-league football always makes me laugh. Not so much at the stadiums, which are endearing, nor the standard of play which is often surprisingly high, but the fans, or more specifically, the fan. This fan is extraordinary. His clothes are what I imagine a fanatical ferry-spotter standing alone at Harwich might wear. His haircut is resolutely mid-1970s, slicked back in the middle and puffed up on the sides. His conversation is littered with references to ungainly places and overladen with obscure statistics. However, on the Spion Kop at Wexham Park, all three steps of it, he is king, and it is his commentary which is listened to. Of course, he is also the club's singer-songwriter, adapting such classics as 'We are Chelsea' so they are relevant to his own club. Just as on a Spanish holiday you might wonder about the past of the electric organist playing in the corner of the bar, I often wonder about the origins of this giant of the non-league scene. One theory I hold is that he used to support a fashionable London club until in a quiet moment during a dull game with most people absorbed in their programmes he tried to start a chant only to be completely ignored. I wouldn't be surprised if such an experience were sufficiently scarring to leave you grateful for non-league football. Alternatively he may merely have been too short to watch football successfully from a cosmopolitan terrace. Whatever his history there is no doubting his position as general of his own army. It may not be much of an army, comprising as it does kids who haven't enough pocket money to be able to afford to watch anyone else and pensioners who have long since ceased caring who they watch. But it cannot be denied that it is an army.

I was interested to note that there had been a coup at Woking and a new general had been installed. This came as a relief, for the last time I watched Woking a couple of Chelmsford generals and their little gang had shimmied into the Woking end in one of the most leisurely and outdated moments of hooliganism I have ever witnessed. It was a bizarre sight, hippies slowly shoving OAPs. Woking had got a draw but Chelmsford had won the fighting and the replay. The new general was definitely of the flawed singer-songwriter rather than the restricted-growth variety and he demonstrated his talent with a tuneless version of 'You're so shit you're worse than Leatherhead'. Just as I was picking up the lyrics, I was shocked and thrilled to notice that Tommy Langley was playing up front for Slough. Now anyone who saw Langley and Mayes leading the Chelsea line with such effortless incompetence in the late 1970s will tell you that when your money is down a thirty-two-year-old Langley (surely he must be older by now, but no) might well be your first choice striker for the opposition. I was less excited by the fact that 'The Pension Shop' was emblazoned across the Woking shirts.

The whistle blew, bringing an end to my reverie. Woking nearly scored in the 1st minute, hit the bar in the 3rd and in the 8th Buzaglo skinned a man on the left, cut inside and stroked the ball into the corner of the net.

'Bet of the decade. I told you buddy, it's the bet of the decade,' screamed Sean the Spread.

'Christ we might have under-egged it on the scores,' said Neighbour.

Mickey lit a Villiger cigar and shouted, 'Hey goalie, what's the score?'

The general got his choirboys going with a rousing rendition of 'Give us a wubble woo . . .'.

This was easy. Woking continued to dominate the game. Scouse and Buzaglo looked murderous in the frontline, Biggins was composing in the middle and Caulfield hadn't even had to use his big hands. The ball hit the back of the Slough net: disallowed. A defender cleared the ball off the line. It was only a matter of time before the next goal.

'Hey number 7 where's your handbag?' guffawed Neighbour, lightening up into artlessness.

Then Langley, of all people, promptly went and equalized. I tore up the 3–0 and 4–0 slips, feeling depressed enough to buy a Westlers only there were none on offer. Half-time came and we had to change ends, a rather touching non-league custom. Halfway round we had a quick piss behind the stands. There was nothing territorial about this you understand, it was just there were no toilets.

Mickey killed his Villiger. 'So a few of our bets are down. But these lads, they're forever drawing or losing at half-time before turning it on in the second half. Remember Clapton? One–nil down and then they win 8–1 scoring six in the last 20 minutes.'

'That Langley's looking a bit useful. . . .' worried Neighbour.

Woking kicked off, and found Buzaglo down the right. He dragged the ball across the area and there was little Scouse nodding the ball towards goal. Was it in? Yes. Mickey was ecstatic and started to jig around the terraces singing, 'We're in the money', while the rest of the crowd chanted the more traditional 'Two one, two one, two one . . .'.

I checked my slips and did some arithmetic. One more goal for Woking equalled £625, two more would bring £2,500, plus £200 for the win bet.

'Come on Woking. Attack, attack, attack! Don't sit on your lead for Christ's sake.' They defended. Time began to pass far too quickly and our incitements became more urgent and more obscure.

'Come on Woking! What about your reputation for attractive football.'

'Woking! Remember Eggy James.'

With barely a cigarette to go before the final whistle Baron hoofed the ball up and Buzaglo sprinted across the half-way line into the clear. He advanced on goal. A one on one. £625, here we go.

The whistle blew. The linesman's flag was raised. Unquestionably this was the worst offside decision of all time. Sean the Spread did his nut, as they say. The Woking players didn't even complain, and 2 minutes later the final whistle blew. Sean the Spread was still ranting when the general approached him.

'Hey chieftain, calm yourself. Sure it was a dodgy decision, but we won, we won 2–1. We stuffed Slough.'

'Dodgy!'

'Who cares? We're in the second round of the Cup. We're on the way to Wembley.'

'I'll lay you 250–1 you don't make it.'

'So, 250–1 against us reaching the Twin Towers after what we've just done. I'll have a piece of that. In fact I'll have a fiver on that.'

'Cheers. I always watch the Cup Final from just behind the Royal Box if you want to collect.'

We were actually confident Woking could trounce anyone on their own patch at Kingsfield but unfortunately they drew Fourth Division Cambridge United away and that was the end of the general's fiver. Within two months the 'bet of the decade' presented itself when Chelsea were drawn at home to Crewe and the bookmakers offered 9–1 against Crewe. Mickey, Sean the Spread and I tucked in with enthusiasm but we were the only people not smiling in the Shed when Chelsea jammed a late equalizer. I haven't had a bet on the Cup since.

Donald Trelford

Donald followed the journalist's classic route to Fleet Street. After Cambridge, he worked on papers in Coventry and Sheffield before going to Africa as a freelance correspondent, and then joining the Observer *in 1966 where he has been Editor since 1975. He is the author of* Snookered *and* Child of Change, *with Gary Kasparov.*

A Smile on the Coventry Face

DONALD TRELFORD

To some, engines, meccano, scientific experiment:
To some, stamps, flowers, the anatomy of insects:
To some, twisting elbows, torturing, sending to
    undeserved Coventry

To some, soldiers, Waterloo, and miniature Howitzers:
To some, football
In the sadness of an autumn afternoon
Studs and mud, the memorable dribble,
Rhododendrons at the back of the net
And the steamy dark gathering over bonfires,
The weight of water from the loosened skies.
And fingers too numb to undo laces.

Alan Ross, 'Boyhood'

It was a bright spring day that I shall never forget – Saturday 16 May
1987. There was political fever in Britain, with Mrs Thatcher
expected to call a general election that very weekend. I looked into her
face for clues as she sat with Denis in the VIP box at Wembley
stadium, with Neil and Glenys Kinnock just a few seats along.

I was there with my father, eating sandwiches, waiting for the
kick-off. I should have been at the office producing the *Observer*, for
Saturday is the busiest day of the week for a Sunday paper. But this
was a rather special occasion – Coventry City's only appearance in the
Cup Final in its 104 years of history.

I should explain that I was born in Coventry and went to the local
grammar school. My parents and my younger sister still live there. For
several seasons in my early teens in the immediate postwar years I
never missed a home game. I kept all the programmes. When my pals
and I couldn't afford to go through the turnstiles at Highfield Road we
used to arrive early and find a way over the wall. This was not easy as I
recall. In fact, a friend of mine cut his little finger so badly on the

broken glass on top of the wall that he still felt the ache many years later when he was playing or coaching rugby at county level. He told me that he used to curse me – for inciting him to juvenile crime – every time the pain came back. Even though I had moved away from home more than thirty years before – to the RAF, to Cambridge, to Sheffield, to Africa and finally Fleet Street – I had never lost touch with Coventry City, or the Sky Blues as I later learned to call them after Jimmy Hill's marketing revolution of the early 1960s. Wherever I was in the world – up Zomba mountain, covering a civil war in the Congo, on a train from Shanghai to Nanking – I always managed to pick up the Saturday scoreline. I went to see them when I could, which wasn't often for a toiler in the Saturday vineyard.

Once, when I was attending a party at the House of Lords, I found myself engaged in conversation with two venerable members of that venerable institution – that is to say, they were slightly older than myself. One of them had been a close confidant of two Prime Ministers and the other had worked as an advisor to successive Chancellors of the Exchequer. But we didn't talk about the goings-on at either Number 10 or Number 11 Downing Street. Instead, we talked football.

The advisor to Prime Ministers had been in his youth an ardent fan of Northampton Town, about which he talked a fair degree of cobblers – so much so that I began to harbour serious doubts about his judgement in other areas of life. Surely, a man who can talk about nothing but Northampton Town must be gravely suspect. His companion, the eminent sociologist, was almost as bad. His obsession was Manchester City, which was something I could understand more readily, since my wife's mother and brother have been infected from an early age with that same mysterious ailment. At many an international conference his mind had strayed from thoughts of the exchange rate of the yen or the European Monetary System to a quagmired goalmouth at Maine Road.

Both of these distinguished men admitted that when they had travelled abroad with the Captains and the Kings, the only information they sought with any urgency from newspapers, radio, television or ticker tape was not the floating value of the pound, or even the latest intelligence from Whitehall, Westminster, Capitol Hill, the Kremlin or the chancellories of Europe – it was the English football results. In particular, wherever they found themselves in the world – in Peking, Bangkok or Bucharest – they followed the fortunes of Northampton Town and Manchester City. One of them said that while he was fer-reting out intelligence about Northampton Town's scorers he always made sure he was properly briefed on any news relating to Huddersfield Town, in case his master, Harold Wilson, the then Prime Minister, might have an urgent need to know.

What struck me about this strange encounter was that neither man had seen these teams play, except perhaps very occasionally when they happened to be on tour in London, for over half a lifetime. Yet they retained a youthful exuberance, a detailed memory for players' names and positions and colourful incidents, as if they were recalling those anguished and delicate moments of their very first love affair – which, in a way, I suppose they were. It occurred to me that there must be scores, maybe hundreds, of famous men in the grip of such childish undiscovered fantasies who were ready, like me and my friends in the House of Lords, to come out of the closet and admit to their secret obsession.

Anyway, there we were at Wembley, my father and I, eating our sandwiches, when he turned to me and said: 'Do you realize when it was that I first took you to see Coventry play Spurs? It must have been forty years ago.' This sombre thought silenced us both, as we cast our minds back to Arthur Rowe's push and run team of the late 1940s: to big Ted Ditchburn in goal, the stylish Burgess and Baily, Duquemin the black-haired centre forward and – most memorable of all – the impossibly neat figure of Alf Ramsey at fullback, who never seemed to get his shorts dirty or disturb his immaculate parting. It's funny, but one has no memory of rain or discomfort or hooligans, though all must have been present at times.

This curious discovery – that I had personally experienced 40 per cent of Coventry's history – stayed with me throughout the match and kept breaking inconveniently into my thoughts as I watched the players on the field. I was reminded of a poem by Alan Ross, the *Observer*'s former cricket correspondent, 'J M Parks at Tunbridge Wells', in which the watching poet's mind in 1951 is taken back to Eastbourne in 1935 when he had seen Jim Parks's father batting in a similar way. The double focus had filled him with inevitable thoughts about the passing of time, of continuity, change and survival. Something of the sort happened to me at Wembley until – like Mr Ross – 'drowning, I struggled to shake off the past'.

Before shaking it off though, I stayed with the father–son theme long enough to recall the only great moment in my father's career. It was among the mining villages of County Durham, where he had been brought up. He described the incident in a letter:

> In 1925, the Waterhouse and Esh Winning show organised a schools' football knock-out to raise money, and the gold medals were on display in the watchmaker's window next to my home in Durham Road. I looked at them every day and wished and wished. The Esh Winning team, for which I played, was in very poor shape. As sometimes happens, we had lost six or seven of the previous year's team as they left school, and we were bottom of the Deerness Valley League. Somehow we scrambled our way to the final and played Waterhouses school. At half-time we were 3–0 down, but somehow we managed to pull level and win 5–4 in extra time. It is one of my great regrets that this medal, the only reason I ever won, was stolen some years later in Coventry.

I have always minded on his behalf. When I first saw Coventry City play, the Cup Final was an impossible dream. To reach the Third Round and meet First Division opponents was enough ambition – and not one that was fulfilled very often. Coventry were in the Second Division in those days, having risen from the Third Division South the year I was born. They had done this with a last-game-of-season victory over Luton Town, led by 'Ten-goal Joe Payne', a feat that was still recounted with civic pride – and a world war – later. As the players walked out onto the perfect, sunlit Wembley turf, it was hard – even for a cricket and rugby addict like me – to doubt the validity of football's claim to be the national game. Flags were flying; happy bright-eyed people were cheering: the passion and the pageantry were things to savour. Football, after its recent ugly scenes of mindless violence, suddenly seemed alive and well and living in England with a smile on its face. Surprisingly, this sense of euphoria and relief, shared by many people at Wembley that day, suffered no disillusion in the two hours or so that followed. As a Coventry fan, I would have remembered every hack and scuffle of a mud-bound punch-up, but thankfully it turned out to be the very opposite: one of the most exciting, skilful and well-mannered finals in living memory.

Jimmy Hill had made Coventry into a modern club and had taken them into the First Division. A succession of unmemorable managers had kept them there, by hook or by crook, for the next two decades, but no cups had been acquired to take back to the city. Now, John Sillett, the former Chelsea fullback and George Curtis, Coventry's crew-cut veteran of a centre half, had formed a lively professional partnership that had lifted the club into the top half-dozen or so teams and propelled them here to Wembley. Big cheery men, bursting out of their suits, they strode onto the pitch like happy children at their birthday party. One of them quipped: 'We always win our last match of the season. We have to – it's usually to avoid relegation.'

Looking at George Curtis and the Coventry defender Trevor Peake, I recognized the standard Coventry face from my childhood. Boys at school looked like that. George Mason, who handed on the number 5 shirt to Curtis, was the first of this strong silent type. Recently, I saw a young crew-cut defender called Dobson on television and knew immediately that he had this same expressionless visage – I checked and found he was born there. This may seem strange, since the Coventry car factories attracted unemployed people from all over Britain – Irish, Welsh, and north-easterners like my father, when they expanded before the war. But there is such a thing as a Coventry face, and I know it when I see it, though my own features are too dark and mobile to qualify.

A curious aspect of this nostalgia for one's home-town football club is that it keeps people in touch with their roots, long after they have moved away in search of other things with which to fill their lives. Very often, as they move on up the social ladder, these memories of queueing and jostling among football crowds are their only vivid recollection of the physical realities of working-class life. One vision I often recall is looking out from my bedroom window at home in the Coventry of my teens and seeing all the men solemnly reversing their small cars out of their garages into the communal back entry at exactly the same time on a Saturday afternoon. It was a ritual, like the carriages going to church in Jane Austen's England, as they set off for the ground in time for the 3 p.m. kick-off.

In the debate on seated sports stadia, I find my mind drawn back with a warm glow to the working-class idyll of Spion Kop at Highfield Road, or hanging from the struts in the stand at Filbert Street in Leicester on Boxing Day, the only place a small boy could perch with a view of the pitch. I sometimes think that the reputations of great players past – Stanley Matthews, for example, or Frank Swift – were partly the product of a folklore tradition in which mighty deeds were reported back through the milling crowds from those at the front to those swaying sightless at the rear. Thus a winger's dribble past two men was extended to four or five in the telling, or a goalkeeper's dive added feet and inches on its relay to the back of the crowd. The instant TV replay has killed off much of this romance.

The Cup Final itself, meanwhile, had got off to quite a start when Clive Allen scored with a diving header inside 2 minutes and Dave Bennett equalized after 10. The Spurs midfield – which could move so quickly into attack – looked formidable: Hoddle and Waddle, those rhyming long-legged magicians, plus Ardiles, Hodge, and Paul Allen. Paul's cousin Clive played, as it were, alone up front and was on target for fifty goals that season. The sight of his bustling around the box, his quick turns and eye for unconsidered trifles took me back to Jimmy Greaves, whom I once saw score five goals at White Hart Lane on a day when he seemed to be breathing a higher grade of oxygen than anyone else. The Spurs defence, though, looked more vulnerable to high crosses aimed at Regis and Houchen from the dancing Bennett and the fizzy Gynn.

Seeing Coventry's strength in the air made me think of Ted Roberts in the old days, who could get up high to the ball, usually from crosses by 'Plum' Warner or Norman Lockhart, but tended to stub his toe when he tried to kick it. Ken Chisholm, a noisy Scottish international of the 1950s, also fired bullets off his head. Some of the current players – Micky Gynn, with his mustachioed air of a 1930s' cad seducer, or skipper Kilcline, more Edwardian with his fierce walrus-like demeanour – could have come from earlier times.

Play swung excitingly from end to end, with a dozen attempts on both goals, until Gary Mabbutt managed to toe in a Hoddle free-kick just before half-time when the giant 'keeper Ogrizovic was unusually slow off his line. He made an interesting contrast to Clemence at the other end – the bull mastiff against the nervy greyhound. Alf Wood, later the Coventry trainer, had been goalkeeper in my time, understudied by the green-jerseyed Peter Taylor, who went on to be Brian Clough's alter ego. The baldheaded Wood never seemed to dive and dirty his yellow jersey in contrast with his gymnastic successor, Reg Matthews, who wore a red one and played for England. I remember seeing Reg play outside right for Barker's Butts Secondary school. He later grew very tall and went in goal.

Looking at Ogrizovic, Kilcline and Regis, a powerful trio, I was reminded of the old saying that a successful team needs three good players – in goal, at centre half and centre forward – and the other pieces will fall into place. This was true of the nucleus of England's World Cup winning team – Banks, Moore and Charlton. Suddenly, even though they were a goal down, I knew Coventry were going to win and I perked up.

The equalizer in the second half – a thundering diving header by Houchen from a Bennett cross – was immortalized on every sports page next morning. A framed colour picture of it hangs in my study as I write. It was one of those beautiful action shots – a man at full stretch with both feet off the ground. To do it at any time would be marvellous – but to have done it in the Cup Final at Wembley must have been one of the greatest moments of Houchen's life. After that, everything else must have been an anti-climax.

The match was settled in extra-time with an own goal by Mabbutt, who thus emulated Turner of Charlton in the 1946 Cup Final by scoring at both ends. It was a sad way for such a match to end, but even Spurs acknowledged afterwards that Coventry, with their driving energy and resilience in coming back twice from behind – deserved their result. It had been such a fast and friendly humdinger that both teams stayed on the pitch for long afterwards, as if they were sorry it had to end.

I thought of the old Coventry players of thirty and forty years ago: how many of them were there to celebrate, or watching on television? Where was George Lowrie, the Welsh centre forward who once scored a goal at a match at West Bromwich Albion (I was there) straight from the kick-off. Or Jack Snape, as fearsome as his name, and Aldecoa, as exotic as his; Harry Barratt, Martin McDonnell, Bryn Allen, Peter Murphy and Iain Jameson.

The victory did wonders for the city, which had been going through hard times. The following week was like a gigantic party. Sober accountants went about in pin-striped suits and blue and white Coventry City caps. The town was draped in banners in the club colours. Team photographs peered out from every shop window. The water in the civic fountains was blue. The Herbert Museum had a display case of commemorative scarves, banners, hats and mugs – 'to preserve the evidence of this event for future generations'. There was even a mini-scandal when a local celebrity was found to have taken his secretary, not his wife, to Wembley in his Rolls Royce, to have drunk champagne in the car park, and then disappeared. His wife sounded as though she was more disappointed at missing the match than losing her husband.

Sadly, the brighter future forecast for the depressed city did not materialize. Neil Kinnock, who had taken hope from the victory of the underdogs at Wembley, failed to score in the general election that followed three weeks after.

Later that same year, for my half-century, my enterprising daughter Sally persuaded the whole of the winning Coventry City football team, led by John Sillett and George Curtis, to sing me 'Happy Birthday'. The video is one of my most prized possessions. Of the few bouquets that life has thrown my way, this one smelt the sweetest.

Tom Watt

Tom is an Arsenal supporter and player-manager of Walford Boys Club, a charity team derived from the 'EastEnders' television series, in which he played Lofty. Other acting credits include The Foreigner *at the Albery Theatre, and* The Cherry Orchard *at the Aldwych. He has also written plays for fringe theatre, and articles for* The Guardian, *and for the fanzine* One Nil Down, Two One Up, *among others.*

Sunday Sport

TOM WATT

Number 6. Tom Watt. Oh dear. The rest of the team spends coach rides home playing Pin The Tail on Tommy Watt. Tries hard and picks the team.

Walford Boys Club programme pen pictures, 1989

There is something very old fashioned about the whole business of charity football: the bus rolling down miles of country lanes; fog lifting slowly off a muddy pitch somewhere in England; fourteen naked men in a tin shed. It should all be shot in black and white. Good intentions, endless mickey taking and children, soaked to the skin as often as not, smiling bravely, autograph books in hand. It could be footage from a 'keep-the-troops-morale-up' one reeler.

It's no coincidence that two or three members of the Walford Boys Club XI are adenoid-perfect in their renditions of Pathe News commentary on the arrival at grounds, knocking in, and the post-match inquest. 'This brave and happy band . . . dozens line the route . . . game that counts . . . tired but satisfied, job well done,' etc. Indeed the hotchpotch nature of the side – the sublime (or at least good semi-pro standard) turning out alongside the ridiculously incompetent – is reminiscent of the war years, when a Mortensen or a Matthews was likely to turn up guesting for the locals against an Army or Pro XI.

Celebrity sides have, I suppose, traditions of their own – through Stan Boardman, Dennis Waterman, the Showbiz XI – which gives the whole territory a beer-belly, baggy-shorts and balding-feel, no matter how smart we may think we look in our new Internazionale strip.

It's fitting then, that one of the Walford Boys Club's stalwarts is Tony Kay, ex-Sheffield Wednesday, Everton and England, who his current team-mates claim to have spotted in grainy monochrome clips from 'History of Association Football' videos. Certainly it is generally agreed that the day Harry Catterick signed Tony from Wednesday –

for a record-breaking £60,000 – was the day Everton made sure of the 1962–3 League Championship. He won his first England cap the following year and looked a good bet to play right half for his country in the 1966 World Cup.

Instead, the infamous Swan/Layne/Kay 'bribery' scandal brought an abrupt end to Tony's professional career: a prison sentence and a life-long ban from the FA. The story is one that has been chronicled elsewhere – a sad, sordid little tale of injustice and compromise. Here, it just needs to be remembered that the same newspaper which would later accuse him of 'throwing' a game between Sheffield Wednesday and Ipswich Town had, on the day itself, awarded A. Kay its man of the match star rating.

Looking back through the cuttings, it's clear the relationship between football and the tabloids was much the same as it is now: obsessive, hysterical and compulsive – like watching a husband and wife throw crockery at one another. Players sold fatuous and self-indulgent stories to reporters who edited them into something resembling pulp fiction. The sensational and often misleading headlines sold papers, which sustained circulation figures through habitual transgression of the boundaries of privacy, propriety and honest reporting, while the newspapers set themselves up as the moral guardians of our national game. Salvoes of accusation and self-righteousness would follow each new set of 'amazing revelations', to which the geriatric football authorities would respond with no trace of the dignity one would expect of their advanced years. Then, as now, it was all very mucky and wantonly unconstructive; a relationship not unlike that between the same tabloids and the casts of popular soap operas today.

Undoubtedly, tabloids and the fact that people want to read them are the problem, but you can hardly complain if you're selling them raw material in the first place. It was disappointing but not surprising, therefore, that on two occasions opponents were offered money – and in one case agreed – to put their names to purple accounts of games against Walford Boys Club. Football and 'EastEnders' – too good a chance to pass up. We'll write it, all you have to do is sign it so we can't be sued. Soaps and soccer probably get the press they deserve. Actors playing football – even if it is to raise money for charity – expect to get caught in the crossfire.

Tony Kay, of course, knows all this better than most – having had his life turned upside down by a dozen misleading columns in the *Sunday People*. But he's still got the Game. Now rumoured to be over 400 years old – though he doesn't look a day over fifty-three – Tony has been a Walford Boys regular for nearly three years. Of course he has to put up with half the team telling him he should be turning out for Age Concern, and the other half suggesting he'd be more at home playing for his local Victoria Wine team. But it's a game every Sunday, competitive but not too quick, and often at grounds and against ex-pros he knew as a young man. To watch Tony in action – red hair bristling like an old loo brush, shins sculpted by Black and Decker, getting to tackles as early as he can – one could get a little sentimental. Fortunately, he's still as loud and objectionable as he was as a professional. He never was a man to ask or give the benefit of the doubt to anyone – team mate or opponent – on a football pitch.

Walford Boys Club. The Arsenal must be held, in part at least, responsible. The community sports scheme at Highbury is not fully integrated or ambitious in comparison to the admirable examples of Spain or Italy, but it is a step in the right direction. Very well managed by a small, full-time staff and a team of trainees, Action Sport is based at the JVC indoor training centre in the executive complex behind the Clock End, and it does much of its best work through outreach projects into local schools and youth clubs. In the early days, someone decided it might be a good idea to involve Lofty from 'EastEnders' in publicizing the new scheme, knowing that Tom Watt would turn up at the opening of an envelope if it had anything to do with Arsenal. One evening I took half a dozen boys from the show to play the Action Sport Staff. Our first defeat.

Over the next few weeks, leading up to a seven-a-side Soaps Cup Tournament for the NSPCC in front of 15,000 at Goodison Park, this all started to seem like a dangerously good idea. We all wish, more or less, secretly, we could have been professional footballers, don't we? And here we are, kicking a ball in a good cause at a famous ground with a crowd watching. Laughter can sound like cheering to the fevered imagination. Nick Berry (Simon Wicks in the series), who had never really recovered after receiving a trophy from Bobby Moore while captain of his school team, was particularly infatuated, as I remember. Fixtures were arranged, the use of the name Walford was cleared with the BBC, kit and boots were browbeaten out of company PR departments and a few relatives and friends, like Tony Kay, were brought in to turn seven actors into a team. Walford Boys Club rushed headlong, gasping for breath, into its first full season.

Strange things happen to an actor when he puts on a football kit. A self-obsessed, bitchy bundle of nerves becomes a self-obsessed, bitchy bundle of nerves with funny-shaped legs. Chris McHallem is an excellent example: a one-time Dexy's Midnight Runners roadie-turned-actor, twice his body weight in long black hair, and double-jointed in so many places he's a certainty for the lead in *Exorcist 7,* this mild-mannered Chelsea fan with a love for black clothing became one of the country's better known faces: Rod, the punk who hides under a bushel in Albert Square. Thirty minutes before kick-off a dark cloud of seriousness settles over the Walford Boys Club right back. It's a look that says: I remind myself of Tony Dorigo. When Chris started turning out for the Walford Boys Club, he'd puff his way through 30 minutes before retiring to the dressing room to recover sufficiently to sign autographs at the end of the game. Such is the power of imagination that after two seasons applying himself to his game with the determination of a pit bull terrier – and given the current crisis of confidence in English fullbacks – Chris probably now *is* Tony Dorigo, or something like him. He lasts the 90 minutes, treats most left wingers with the contempt they deserve and has a profound understanding of the offside principle – the last a prerequisite for our aging back four. First name on the team sheet and completely reliable. McHallem won't miss his football even if he has to get up from a sick bed – or anyone else's bed – to play.

Oh yes. Bed. And getting people out of it. The Walford Boys Club plays between thirty-five and forty games a year. That's every Sunday save a two-month break over the winter when our crowds can catch real pantomime. So every Sunday morning has that little extra excitement about it. Will eleven get up? The tension is particularly keen when its a 9 a.m. start for a game in Dorset or Shropshire. No matter how calm I've decided to be the night before, it invariably comes down to desperate phone calls an hour after planned departure time; a little cajoling, a little pleading, a little more blackmail. Only once in over 100 games have we turned up a player short. But at times it does feel like I've been set up: Gary Macdonald sits around the corner, engine running, waiting for me to panic while everyone else gets another cup of tea and enjoys the drama.

Eventually, we gather. From all over London, obviously. But this Sunday, for example, Steve Ashton (Omo in 'EastEnders') has to drive up from rep in Plymouth and Rob Hudson (Yorkie in 'The Bill') was on the town in Sheffield last night. What has a distressed backstreet in Finsbury Park done to deserve this? Bodies pile out of cars into the flat. In minutes the place is awash in coffee and fast break-fasts. In the front room, the arguments start over a football video, *Lost In Space*, or *Public Enemy*. A queue forms to use the phone, a tradition so ancient that people now save calls up for Sunday morning at Tom's house. Then like a plague of locusts, at a word, they're gone. The coach has arrived and we're away.

The coach. The *deus ex*'s own *machina*. All we need. From the outset I never wanted money to change hands. No expenses, no petrol money: just send a coach for us and we'll be there and that's how it works. Organizers know where they stand, and can usually blag a free or cut-rate bus, and none of the money paid at the turnstiles ends up in anybody's pocket. And we have a surprise to look forward to each week. Will it be the Scottish National team bus? A retired number 210? The school holiday coach? Or sixteen men in a twelve-seater transit? A cassette player is a plus, a coffee machine is greeted with delight and a video means you'll have trouble getting the team off at the other end.

As we're negotiating the driver out of unfamiliar territory and onto the open road, the various travel groups organize. The card school huddles around whatever resembles a table. The actor chappies – those who've left or are about to leave the comfortable security of a long-running series – are at the back, exchanging professional gossip before moving onto serious discussion of romance at its most lurid and bizarre. The Sunday readers and the sleepers settle somewhere in between. And the debating society, of course, can come to life anywhere and eventually takes in all corners of the now fast-moving vehicle.

In the chair Mr Dennis Valentine, who takes it upon himself to ensure that any discussion steers a course well away from that of recognizable logic and is not allowed to drop from the level of a strangled shout. Should distraction flag during the course of a long run out of London there are deputies ready to urge the chairman into loud and abrasive action: Dennis, man, perhaps you should room with Tony Kay? Perhaps you're not God's gift to women? Perhaps Sid Owen can outsprint you over 30 metres? Dennis was the Walford Boys Club Sports Personality of the Year 1988 and no one has seen or even enquired of the trophy since. Without him a ramshackling outfit such as our own would have trouble ramming or shackling. He bears a striking resemblance, in looks and manner, to a hungover Eddie Murphy and demands the same kind of attention. In a team full of people who claim to entertain others for a living, Dennis, it soon becomes clear, is the one who ought to be paid for what he does in public. Thank you speeches delivered in strict Ragamuffin styling, dance routines, storytelling, wild accusations of a deeply personal nature and even something resembling song. Whether he's going to be playing or on the bench he's completely committed to the Idea and, therefore, Will Be There. Nobody's quite sure quite what Dennis does the rest of the week, but he's a star on Sunday.

I'm sure that anyone who has ever dreamt Sunday Football dreams would understand why the Boys Club seems like the best thing since diving headers. Were my memory to serve me that well I'd be tempted to catalogue the ninety or so grounds we've played on over the last three years. There's the total wish fulfilment of playing at a palace like Villa Park (against *Football Today* magazine) – if we played on that surface every week, we'd always win 5-0, wouldn't we? So who shall I be while we're playing today? Peter Simpson? David O'Leary? Jeff Blockley, more like. Or it's Griffin Park just before Christmas. Steve Perryman's got a side up, all ex-pros who you've paid good money to watch in their time. Do you just follow Trevor Brooking around all afternoon because you're so proud to be on the same pitch with him? Or do you wait for the first good tackle and mutter: 'That's for the 1980 Cup Final.'? Or we're at VS Rugby ankle deep in mud against a Barry Powell XI with over 7000 packed into a tiny ground. When you know that's more than watched Manchester United play there in an FA Cup tie, it lends the game a certain edge. All thoughts of the day job are left on the touchline.

The match, like the build-up, is all about imagination. While Chris McHallem is Tony Dorigo, Gary Macdonald imagines he's Johnny Barnes. Before a very successful career as an actor, including a year as

Darren in 'Eastenders', Gary played a lot of semi-pro football around the south east: Leatherhead, Epsom and Ewell, Southall, and Barnet. He's a gifted player – strong, good balance, a bit of pace and a great first touch. Gary's a regular scorer for us at centre forward or from midfield. Having made the choice to pursue acting as his career, he still has a stage on which to play out the 'might have been'. To ensure the competitive edge to games that can motivate the rest of us through a whole season, a side like ours needs players of his ability. Just one problem. The John Barnes thing. Do I have to sign Peter Beardsley before 'Macca' will pass to another Walford boy?

Gary Macdonald could also eat for England. The post-match charity football reception is an institution in itself. I suspect those particular sausage rolls and that Black Forest gâteau follow us around the country. I don't know what clubrooms look like when they're not jammed with footballers, their partners, kids and club officials. To give you the full picture, I would have to talk to Tony Kay, whose desire to be at the bar when the first cork is pulled seems to win out over the idea of a shower after the game. For my part, my body's in a state of shock after 90 minutes' agitation and public humiliation; it takes a while for systems to stabilize before I can face the cheese and pineapple cubes and orange squash. But I'll not miss the speeches. The club secretary, the charity organizer, and, of course, our own larger-than-life Mr Dennis Valentine. Jokes, cheers and little trophies all round. We're back to that wartime one-reeler.

The reception has its own presiding spirit. A sense of warmth and human fellowship between strangers that moves gently, inexorably, around the room. The spirit has a name: Ed Joyce, known to us as Shades. It is the nature of this kind spirit to be all things to all men at your choice of social gathering. Ed is a social worker – my social worker, the story goes; though he's currently employed by the London Borough of Westminster. We go back a long way. As far as football goes, back to a Charlie Nicholas goal against Chelsea in 1986, nutmegging Doug Rougvie and chipping the 'keeper from 35 yards out. Now Ed's got the season ticket next to mine at Highbury and his involvement with Walford Boys Club was inevitable. Ed's back heels remain the stuff of legend. He was the first man to score for us in front of a crowd, continues to charm for Walford and England and looks very smart in a big overcoat. Frustrated, no doubt, by not getting a regular game for us, Ed's answer was to train for the 1989 New York Marathon, which he duly completed in 3 hours 41 minutes. Mighty shades. Like I say, a presiding spirit.

The Walford Boys Club always turns out at least six or seven well-known faces. We don't leave until everyone's had their photos taken and their autograph books signed. But the football. Are we any good? The nature of the beast is that the team's an awkward mix. Quality players: Gary Macdonald, his brother Tony (who's played in goal for Millwall and Brentford reserves); Jason Watkins (last seen in Mike Leigh's movie *High Hopes*), who used to play wide right for Wrexham; Barry Nix who captained England Schoolboys fifteen years ago, and Tony Kay. Players who'd look good in decent Sunday League sides: Gary Webster (Graham in 'EastEnders'), Mark Burdis (Stewpot in 'Grange Hill'), who played for Islington schoolboys; Tony Warren (Sticks) who with no Equity card works more often than most of us who have one; Nick Berry, Rob Hudson, Mr Valentine. Then there are the others like myself, Chris and Sid Owen (Ricky in 'EastEnders') who have little more than a boundless enthusiasm for the game. Like I say, an awkward mix. One that works from time to time, that used to work more often when enough of us were on the same BBC schedule to make regular training feasible. Well, that's my excuse, and I'm sticking to it.

Mind you, when we do train the coaching is of the best. Paul Davis of Arsenal and England may now regret the day he ever heard of Walford. Always ready to make us sweat on a Tuesday night if his perfect left foot is not being put to good use by the mighty Reds, his presence on a Sunday gives the day a sense of *gravitās*. After a few words of encouragement before the kick-off, Paul's face will tell the 90 minutes' story from the touchline. Anticipation, hope, joy, satisfaction, pride, care, irritation, frustration, annoyance, hurt, disbelief, dismay and despair. Two–nil up at half-time, we've lost 3–2.

Over the past three years the Boys Club has raised around £750,000 for dozens of local and national charities. Our opposition chooses where the money goes. The success of the matches stands on the hard work and organization of dedicated individuals who at some point were naive enough to imagine a game against us might be a 'nice idea'.

I suspect what keeps the whole thing going, particularly from the players' point of view, are the overnights. The glamour fixtures – Isle of Wight, Jersey, Scotland – for which travel on a Saturday night and a stopover is required. They are the carrots which get everyone out of bed on time for the weeks preceding them, when it's announced there are only fifteen plane seats booked. One week, I'm scraping together eleven players for a long coach trip to Norfolk; the next, it seems, anyone who has ever played for us is suddenly available and ready for a game. Funny how it works. But not surprising. The movie, I suppose, would be entitled 'Carry On Boys'. Out come the beach wear and the travellers cheques. Heathrow littered with over-sized children in identical romper suits; the Edinburgh shuttle, say, takes on the atmosphere of a Club 18–30 charter. The evening out when we get there invariably encompasses the best and the worst: inspired lunacy that leaves our hosts open-mouthed in appreciation and disbelief; intermittent rallies of very funny, very regressive gags and practical jokes; and bedroom farce of such awkwardness, unsophistication and complexity one mourns the passing of the Ealing Film Comedy from which the whole business obviously takes its cue. Lucky indeed the team that has to play us the day after the night before.

What is the Walford Boys Club really all about? Good works? Group dynamics? The pursuit of the Perfect Game? No. It's very simple. Sunday with the Boys Club is the best crack going.

Eamonn McCabe

After twelve years working for the Observer Eamonn spent a year with Bradford City FC while undertaking a fellowship at the National Museum of Photography, Film and Television. He had previously trained in film studies at San Francisco state college then ran his own agency. He is now picture editor of The Guardian and on Sundays turns out for Battersea.

A Life in the Year
of Bradford City

EAMONN McCABE

I'm feeling happier. Goals cheer you up.

Ian Rush

Bradford City *v* Tottenham Hotspur in the FA Cup. The chance of
an upset in front of a full house at Valley Parade. For the Bradford fans,
mingled with their excitement before the kick-off, there was the worry
that Tottenham's internationals might simply do their job properly,
and earn their Cup bonus by stuffing the home team from the Second
Division. But if Bradford did score first it would, for the fans, be the
best moment of the season – and that was what I wanted to record on
camera.

I crouched down on the gravel track by the sidelines and directed
my lens at the heart of the Kop. Some of the supporters noticed me,
but as the players came out they were soon distracted. This was the
Cup, they had no time for me, or anything else, but the twenty-two
players.

The celebration captured on the cover of *Saturday's Boys* was the
greatest moment for the Bradford City supporters during the 1988–9
season. It was the second after they had taken the lead against
Tottenham. It shows the joy and ecstasy of a goal, celebrated by three
generations of supporters. These are the times that supporters everywhere cherish. Anyone who has ever been to see their team in a really
big match – and seen them win – knows that feeling. For football fans,
that is what Saturdays are about.

I was just pleased to be able to get the shot. It worked. Taking
pictures wasn't always so successful.

'Take another picture with that camera and I'll shove it up your arse.'
These were the first words Mick Kennedy, one of soccer's hard men,

201

said to me as I began to record a year in the life of Bradford City FC, from January 1988 to January 1989. The venue was the team bus travelling to a derby at Sheffield United (there are an awful lot of derbies in Yorkshire). I was recording a day in the life of a football team playing an away match: the meeting at the car park, the pre-match lunch, watching brainless game shows on television to fill in an hour before kick-off, and the arrival at the ground. It was my first day out with the team and it had not started well. At the lunch I was trying to get some pictures of the whole team eating at what seemed a very ceremonial occasion. I crouched down to get a better angle and bang! A door hit me in the small of the back, as a waitress pushed her way through with a tray full of food. Of course the team howled with laughter, as I lay sprawled on the floor.

I was spending a year with Bradford City, on a project for the National Museum of Photography, Film and Television, based in the city. I had been offered a fellowship and along with a teaching commitment I had to produce an exhibition and City were my subject. During my years working as a sports photographer for the *Observer* I had had to act as an action photographer every Saturday, even if I had far more pictorial freedom than many of my colleagues sitting alongside. The fellowship gave me the freedom to point my camera away from the pitch, and my goal was to put up forty pictures at the end of the year without a football in any photograph – everyone knows what a ball looks like. I weakened – there were three in the end.

My intention was to show how an average Second Division football club went about its business. It would have been too easy to choose Liverpool, Manchester United or my own favourites, Spurs (this is currently under review due to the antics of Gascoigne). The glamour of these clubs would have dominated the photographs. The familiar faces of the star players would have prevented the viewer from seeing what it is really like. I wanted pictures of what goes on behind and under the stands; I wanted dirty underwear, not pop star banality. The dreadful fire which killed so many in 1985 was not part of my brief. It happened three years before I arrived and it would have been out of context to include any reference to it. I didn't choose Bradford because of the fire but because the Museum happened to be in Bradford and City fitted the average football club image I was after. The biggest problem I had was being outnumbered: there were always twelve or so of them and only one of me, and they all knew each other so well. Each time I made it into the dressing room I had to overcome the clickey humour and the showing-off tendencies of a few players who thought it was great fun to play up to the camera. I wanted to be a fly on the wall, I did not want set-up pictures of grown men larking around with thumbs up to the camera. Many were nervous and this, in the beginning, came over as aggression, and as I was in their space I did not feel I could push my weight around. I wanted to keep my options open, as I always felt there would be a game in which I would really want to get into this inner sanctum, perhaps after a Cup defeat or when they had won promotion to the First Division, as they so nearly did.

Kennedy's first words to me on the coach made me feel the task of getting close to the players was going to be hard. They were dressed in suits (footballers are always in one uniform or another), reading dossiers on the Sheffield United players on the short motorway journey down to south Yorkshire. Kennedy looked like a college lecturer smoking a pipe as he read his notes on whom to mark, as if he didn't know already. This was a new picture and not one you would expect to see of a man with a reputation as a tough guy on the field. I felt excited as I moved behind him to capture the scene. Then he told me what he was going to do with my camera. It's strange, only one other player has told me where he was going to shove my camera, and that was my great hero Jimmy Greaves. It happened after he had to come off in a game playing for Chelmsford City after his back had gone. I went with Frank Keating from *The Guardian* to see how the great man was coping with life in the lower leagues. Funny how both players knew where to put the camera; perhaps it's part of their media-awareness training.

Things got better with Kennedy, though. Luckily I ran into him one night when he was staying in the same hotel as me in Bradford, waiting to move into a house in the area. I don't think I would have recognized him if he hadn't been wearing another of the uniforms, the smart club tracksuit. We got talking and it turned out his father was born just up the coast from my mother in the west of Ireland. At last I had something in common with a member of the team. (It was certainly never going to be my football skills which at the time were still being paraded on various park pitches on Sunday mornings for Nine Elms

Dynamos, not named after the south London district but after nine elm trees in the garden of one of our founding members.) Kennedy is a much better player than people give him credit for, despite his reputation as a hard man. His quick thinking at a free-kick knocked Spurs out of the FA Cup, on a strange day for me because I wanted both sides to win – one for better pictures, the other for my own supporter satisfaction. In the end I was pleased Spurs lost 1–0: the pictures were great and I was annoyed at how Venables's team of Waddle and company thought they could walk it.

Many things I encountered at Bradford were familiar and to be expected – I had a good idea already of the routines of a football club, but two things did surprise me. The first was that a club in an area of such high immigration should have only one black player on its books. Perhaps it's true that Asian kids are just not into football. The other thing that astounded me was the nomadic life of the professional footballer. Kennedy has in fact had two more clubs since I photographed him – Leicester and Luton – making seven in all. Stuart McCall (the captain) and John Hendrie left after narrowly missing Division One. McCall is at Everton and Hendrie went to Newcastle but now plays for Leeds. There were so many changes as I was finishing the project that I couldn't find anyone I knew to open the exhibition at the museum, as all the players I had decent photographs of had gone.

That good personalities make good pictures is one of the maxims of photo-journalism. Terry Dolan, boss at Valley Parade for most of the time I was there, may be a great manager but he doesn't make many pictures. He is a quiet, unassuming man, who likes to watch his football from the stand, not an easy place to get pictures from. After missing out on promotion to the First Division the previous year and with the results not going too well, he was sacked despite Cup victories over Spurs and Everton, to be replaced by the effervescent Terry Yorath who made more pictures in his first game than Dolan did in nearly a whole year. Yorath is a tracksuited manager who likes to be close to the action. Sitting in the dugout, he leaps up and screams instructions, playing every ball with his players, gesturing to referees and agonizing when things go wrong. But Dolan's quiet authority was more effective – Yorath lost his job in March, as Bradford were struggling in the bottom three. Dolan's new team, unfashionable

Rochdale on the other side of the Pennines, had a fine run to the Fifth Round of the FA Cup and rose rapidly up the Fourth Division.

Bradford's fans have a character all their own. There is a small group of about twelve who sit in the main stand wearing French-style berets in the club colour of claret. They are a passionate lot and organize games against visiting teams' supporters in the morning before the clubs play at Valley Parade. After the morning match they all have a drink together and admire each other's scarves and badges in good humour. During the big match if they think an opposition player has fouled one of their own to a man they bring out a red or yellow card to indicate to the referee what punishment he should dish out. This was one photograph I never got as it never looked quite right in black and white, which is how I chose to record the year. However it is a fond memory of a group of very individual supporters.

There were many moments of high drama: the beating of two First Division teams in the Cups and especially the two games against the great rivals from Middlesbrough in the First Division play-off games. Bradford made a mess of the home leg and didn't score enough goals. The away leg was like a cup final: full house, floodlights giving the pitch a theatrical glow and the fans baying at each other. City lost after extra time. The team were in tears as Dolan gathered the players together and brought them to the end where the Bradford fans were. It made great pictures but I felt desperately sad for them; seeing grown men cry is never easy and for some this was a realization that they were never going to play in the First Division. On that day I came up against one of life's awkward bastards, the steward, sometimes known as 'Jobsworth': 'I can't let you in there mate, it's more than my job's worth.' I had cleared it with Terry Dolan that win, lose or draw I would be able to get into the dressing room after the game as the scenes were bound to be very emotional. Unfortunately no one had told the Middlesbrough steward, so I'll never know what went on behind that door. The silence was deafening.

Index